SIX RINGS

FROM NOWHERE

BIG TALK PUBLISHING, LLC
AURORA, ILLINOIS

For Bulk / Wholesale Purchases Go To:
www.BigTalkPublishing.com

To Book Don Beebe For An Event Go To:
www.DonBeebe.com

To Order Leon Lett / Don Beebe DVD – Super Bowl 20th
Anniversary Documentary Film Go To: www.BigTalkFilms.com

www.SixRingsFromNowhere.com

TABLE OF CONTENTS

A FEW OF DON BEEBE'S ENDORSEMENTS

"*Six Rings From Nowhere* is about a man I have come to greatly admire and respect."

LEON LETT – *Super Bowl XXVII ; "THE PLAY"* ; 3-Time Super Bowl Champion; 2 Pro Bowls; 50 Greatest Cowboys

"Don Beebe is the perfect example that you're never too small if your heart is big."

DONALD TRUMP – *Businessman / TV's The Apprentice*

"We would have never won Super Bowl XXXI without Don Beebe."

BRETT FAVRE – *NFL QB ; 11 Pro Bowls ; 3 MVPs*

"Don Beebe showed what a fighting heart is all about. He gave everything he had all the time."

MARV LEVY – *Hall Of Fame Coach / General Manager*

"Don Beebe played the game the right way both on and off the field."

JIM KELLY – *NFL Hall Of Fame QB*; 4 Pro Bowls

"In Proverbs 16:9 Soloman says, 'The heart of a man plans his way, but The Lord directs his steps'. Don was determined in his heart to lead a life of success, and on his way The Lord gave him some really fast feet! Don was a great teammate and a better friend."

JAMES LOFTIN - *NFL Hall Of Fame Receiver; 8 Pro Bowls*

SIX RINGS FROM NOWHERE
A TRUE STORY OF FAITH, HOPE AND TRIUMPH

From the time he was a rambunctious kid throwing around a football in the backyard of his home in a small Illinois town, Don Beebe harbored a dream a whole lot bigger than his size: to play in the NFL.

And he never let go of that dream, even when he dropped out of college to hang aluminum siding with his brother-in-law.

Even when he was an undersized wide receiver playing football for an undersized school in a remote corner of Nebraska.

Even when he ran in tattered shoes, going head to head with superstars like Deion Sanders, at the NFL Combine.

That's because the one thing Beebe had going for him, besides his incredible speed, was a deep faith. Following Christ's message and a series of life lessons, some harder to learn than others, Beebe realized that when the odds are stacked against you, never give up.

Never. Ever.

Don Beebe not only went on to play nine seasons in the NFL, he earned a record six Super Bowl rings, including four with Jim Kelly's Buffalo Bills and two with Brett Favre's Green Bay Packers.

Beebe's name was also forever etched in the hearts of NFL fans everywhere following Super Bowl XXVII. There, after making a split-second decision that changed the course of his life, he ran down Dallas Cowboys' Leon Lett in an end zone play that would become one of ESPN's top moments in NFL history.

"Six Rings from Nowhere" is the inspiring story of a young athlete's journey of faith and determination that took him from construction worker to NFL record-holder. It is a story of courage … of hope.

It is a story that not only will make you want to stand up and cheer, but begin your own race toward goals that define you as a winner.

Coach Vince Lombardi

"Courage doesn't just appear. It comes only through character, great effort and above all, sacrifice. Football is a lot like the game of life. It requires perseverance, self-denial, hard work, dedication and respect.

But boys, playing in a Super Bowl will define you forever."

Coach Vince Lombardi

INTRODUCTION

By Jim Kelly

NFL Hall of Fame QB

As a quarterback in the NFL, I had the knack of being able to put guys where I thought they could best be used. From the first time I saw Don Beebe working out with the team, I knew he was the kind of player I wanted in my huddle. From the start, you could see his incredible work ethic. You could tell he wanted to be the best he could possibly be. Don had that certain quality. All he needed was the opportunity to show what he could do, and I wanted to give him that opportunity. Athletes with that kind of integrity simply want a chance to prove what they can do. I know that feeling. Yet, when given that opportunity, you have to be able to perform. Don did that, and he did it in such a way we all knew he was special. He was the kind of player that a quarterback, a team and all the fans could pull for.

Don wasn't your typical NFL wide receiver, either. But with that incredible speed and ability to run routes, he could totally embarrass his opponents. He was also such a darn good guy with a remarkable way of communicating so that people listened. It's not that he would voice his opinion. It's the way he went about doing things. Don was a down to earth guy who made his mark quietly ... and always with integrity.

I used to kid Don that if we ever won a Super Bowl he'd have to have a beer with me. He finally did win a championship, but not with the Bills. And the first time I saw him after that Green Bay win, he said to me, "You know why I've got this ring, Jim? Because Favre never threatened me with a beer to get it."

I still smile when I think of that response. It sums up who Don Beebe is. He had a great sense of humor; great work ethic. And most importantly, he never strayed from his beliefs. Don was a role model on and off the field. His story says it all.

FORWARD

By Brett Favre

We would not have won Super Bowl XXXI without Don Beebe. Of course, we had a lot of guys step up, but you have to mention Don as soon as you mention anyone else … His perspective is so good, it's not surprising he always seemed to be one of the players who stepped forward for the big games, or picked up a team when the chips were down.

Don got along with everyone, which helped him fit in quickly when he got to Green Bay. He's such a good person that it almost got overlooked what a good football player he really was. He hustled, which everyone knew about from watching him in Super Bowl XXVII. He was our fastest receiver in Green Bay, and we had some fast ones. He knew how to run good routes, and he had really good hands. Of course, he knew how to get open, which was important. He was really a unique player because he could do so many things. Our friendship meant a lot to me, although half the time I'd ask him to play golf, he couldn't because he was doing something with his wife Diana or with his kids. He's such a great family man, a great role model.

Everyone who knows Don Beebe's name knows he's a deeply Christian man. On the one hand, he's not afraid to talk about it to anyone, and he speaks to a lot of groups about his faith. On the other hand, he knows when not to push it, because that can turn someone off. Guys in the locker room weren't afraid to be themselves around Don, although everyone has a lot of respect for him. Don just wanted people to know that Christianity is there for them. The way he handled it made people respect him even more.

A COACH'S PERSPECTIVE

By MARV LEVY

NFL HALL OF FAME COACH

I have really good memories of Don. He gave everything he had all the time. He was a tremendous competitor. He was a perfect fit on the football field with the rest of the cast we had. He certainly complimented James Lofton, Andre Reed, and Pete Metzelaars; and of course, Jim Kelly and Thurman Thomas, the other skill position players.

When Don broke his leg against Miami, he came back and was as fast as he was before. Not only did he show the world what a fighting heart is about, he exhibited what the Buffalo Bills were about. No matter how bad the situation, we don't give in.

Marv
Levy

ACKNOWLEDGMENTS

I have lived my life by the 4 F's; faith, family, friends, then football. I will say my thanks in order for this book, as well.

Faith - Without my faith in Jesus Christ I am nothing, but with God I have everything. He has brought me through some tough but exciting times in my life. He blessed me with the best wife in Diana and the best four kids, (Amanda, Chad, MaKayla and Kaitlyn) that a man could ever ask for. In my 40 years of having a relationship with Jesus, he has never let me down and I have never known a life without him. Thank you Lord for giving me eternal life, plus bestowing me with an awesome wife and four children. That leads me to my second most important thing in my life.

Family - For 43 years my dad, mom, two sisters Beth and Diane and two brothers Dan and Dave have taken a fishing vacation to northern Minnesota without missing a single year. Now that is family! It is the best two weeks of the year. From the original seven, it has grown to forty-one people, including our wonderful spouses, our children and our children's kids. And every member of the Beebe family has a relationship with Jesus Christ. Praise God.

Friends - There are too many to mention, but all of you know I love you deeply and want to say thanks for all the great memories we have shared. May God richly bless you. I look forward to the day we will all be together again.

Football - I asked God when I was seven years old to let me be something special in sports. In my wildest dreams I never thought I would be good enough to be in the NFL, but that is why we can't give up faith on Christ. If God lays something on your heart, DON'T EVER GIVE UP ON HIM.

* Thanks so much for letting me share my story. A special thanks to Denise Crosby and Jim Gibson for taking on this project and putting in so many hours to see this come true. May the Lord bless you both.

MR. RALPH C. WILSON JR.

Founder / Owner – Buffalo Bills – NFL Hall Of Fame

"Don Beebe was fast! People will always remember the effort he put forward on that Leon Lett play which reflects on the fact that he never gave up even though the odds were heavily against him."

Proverbs 3:5-6

"Trust In The Lord With All Your Heart And Lean Not On Your Own Understanding; In All Your Ways Submit To Him, And He Will Make Your Paths Straight."

PROLOGUE

As he stepped from the tunnel into the brilliant stadium sunlight, the chunk of anxiety sitting in his gut melted like crushed ice on August asphalt. And Don Beebe smiled. A little boy's dream was about to unfold in the next few hours, and he would have the best seat in the house — between the freshly painted hash marks of an immaculate grass field — as the Buffalo Bills were set to take on the Dallas Cowboys in Super Bowl XXVII. The game would be watched by more than 130 million fans, a fact not lost on Beebe as his gaze took in the surreal panorama stretched out before him.

After a surprisingly restful night, Beebe had taken the first bus from the Hyatt Regency so he could savor every minute of this experience. Dressed in gray cut-off T-shirt and white game pants, the red stripe snaking down the sides, Beebe strolled onto the field knowing that today — January 31, 1993 — was going to be special. This match-up would not only break the Bills' dismal Super Bowl losing streak, he felt certain it would help define his own career that had already been anything but ordinary.

Six years earlier, Beebe had been hanging aluminum siding for his brother-in-law and wondering if he would ever get the chance to play a game of football that involved more than a high school field or suburban backyard. Now, at age twenty-nine and with only four years in the NFL, the five-foot-ten-inch wide receiver was about to take the field for his third Super Bowl. Even now, saying the numbers seemed surreal. Four years in the NFL. Three Super Bowls. No championship ring yet, but that was about to change.

After all, everyone agreed Jim Kelly was the better quarterback —
certainly the more experienced. And no matter what the bookies in
Vegas said, the Bills' defensive line had the size and quickness to
corral Emmitt Smith. Besides, the real odds were on their side. How
can you get to the Super Bowl three times in a row without taking
home a title?

Beebe ignored the camera flashes that were already popping
like dandelions in a neglected Little League outfield. He strolled
along the parameters of the stadium, soaking in the Southern
California sun that somehow made the turf appear too perfect to be
natural. He walked to the middle of the field, where Frank Reich
called out to him.

"Bro, over here …let's throw a few so I can start warming up
my arm." The lanky backup quarterback lobbed a lazy spiral to
Beebe, who caught it easily with one hand, then just as effortlessly
flipped it back to his teammate. The two men, roommates on the
road and best friends no matter where they were playing, settled into
a familiar warm-up, words unnecessary as the minutes ticked off and
anxious fans began to pepper the stands. Beebe had played in plenty
of arenas much bigger and grander than this hundred-year-old
stadium. But despite the cracked masonry and antiquated locker
rooms, he felt goose bumps. "Amazing," he whispered to himself.
"Absolutely amazing."

Grabbing one final pass from Reich, this one with some zip
to it, Beebe dropped the ball to his side and walked toward the

center of the field. In less than an hour this stadium would be filled with a roaring sea of fans, including a couple rows of family and friends from Sugar Grove, Illinois.

Beebe knelt on the freshly painted rose that blossomed in the middle of the fifty-yard-line. He lowered his head. "Lord, this day is yours. Whatever happens in the next few hours, let me glorify your name."

Opening his eyes, he stared for a moment at his white Nike cleats, brand spanking new with a red rose insignia on the right foot. He thought about the shoes he'd worn during his tryout with the NFL — old fishing sneakers with a hole in one toe and soles so loose, they flapped when he ran.

Don felt his eyes moisten. Surprised at the emotion now surging through his body, he knew this was a moment in time he would not ever forget. The former tin man was playing for the NFL championship in the Rose Bowl, the field of his childhood dreams.

* * *

Two-and-a-half hours later, that dream had spiraled into a nightmare. It was the fourth quarter of Super Bowl XXVII and the Bills were getting their lunches handed to them. Beebe wondered if he was the only one who could barely bring himself to look at the scoreboard: 52-17.

What had started as a showdown with barnburner potential — the teams traded touchdowns and turnovers in the first six minutes of the game — was now heading toward an embarrassing rout. From the first quarter on, Jim Kelly was rocked by the Cowboys' defensive line. And the Bills were on their way to racking up a record nine turnovers, even as their defense continued to get trampled by the Troy Aikman-Emmitt Smith juggernaut.

Late in the fourth quarter, Kelly exited the game with a knee injury and Frank Reich stepped in to take his place. No matter what the scoreboard said, the fans were still in their seats, and Beebe was not about to pack it in.

With four minutes, thirty-two seconds left, the clock had become their enemy. "Throw it to me deep, Frank," he told his buddy as the quarterback huddled his offense. "You know I can beat this guy." Reich had heard that same request dozens of times from his best friend. His reply was almost always the same. "You got it, Beebs."

As the ball was snapped on the Dallas thirty-two yard line, Beebe took off running a fly pattern down the left sideline, hoping Reich would be able to break away from the Cowboys line and find the few seconds he needed to drop one into Don's hands. But the bad news only continued.

When he glanced back from the twenty-yard line, he saw his friend scrambling, with Dallas defensive end Jim Jeffcoat bearing down on Reich. "Slow it down, slow it down," Beebe told himself, as he turned back toward the quarterback in hopes of finding a spot where Reich could make the connection.

Too late. Jeffcoat stripped the ball from Reich and it fell at the feet of six-foot-six, 292-pound defensive tackle Leon Lett.

The future two-time Pro-Bowler was only in his third NFL season, but he was having the game of his life, already recording a sack, a fumble recovery and a forced fumble. Spotting gold again, he scooped up the ball with his big hands and headed toward the end zone with defensive tackle Jimmie Jones as his escort.

The groan that arose from Bills fans in the old stadium only confirmed the obvious. It would be an easy six points for Dallas. But Beebe, forty yards away, didn't see it quite that way.

It was not so much a decision as it was a reaction. *There's no way I can catch him,* he thought. It didn't matter. Beebe took off running. With all eyes on Lett rumbling toward the end zone, no one in the stadium noticed the small wide receiver streaking down the right side of the field in pursuit. The three characteristics that had taken Beebe from a job in aluminum siding to a career in the NFL were his tenacity, his blazing speed and his unwavering faith in God. At least two of the trio were on display now.

Hugging the sideline, he blew by the other players as if they were standing still. As Lett passed the ten yard line, Beebe was already at the fifteen. But as the wide receiver drew nearer to the lumbering lineman, Beebe began to question his decision. *Ok, Mr. Hot Shot. You may end up catching this big bull. But how are you gonna take him down?*

He thought about jumping on Lett's back, but the lineman pulled his own surprise. At the eight yard line, Lett, anticipating his first NFL touchdown, couldn't help but showboat, and held the ball out on his right side. With just a couple yards remaining, Beebe saw his opportunity.

He reached out and whacked Lett's hand. The ball fell from the lineman's grip and shot out of the end zone.

As Beebe fell to the ground, Lett stumbled over him, kneeing Don's helmet before landing on the ground himself. The stadium erupted with wild applause, shrieks of laughter, wails of despair and a barrage of four-letter words. Beebe heard none of it. Nor was he aware of Lett, now face down and folded over on his knees in the end zone.

"And look at Lett," boomed NBC's Dick Enberg from the broadcast booth. "If they call that a no-touchdown, he's going to dig a hole and crawl out of this place.''

Don was hardly in a mood to celebrate. Tearing off his helmet, Beebe jogged to the sideline. His back was to the huddle of striped shirts near the fifteen-yard-line still trying to determine just how they would call this unusual turn of events.

"Nice hustle, Beebs!" offered nose tackle Mike Lodish as Don, struggling to collect his breath, took a seat on the bench.

"They gotta rule that a fumble," offered running back Thurman Thomas. "Sure looked like you knocked it out of his hand before he hit the end zone."

Three minutes later, the refs officially agreed, declaring the play a touchback, and handing the ball to the Bills on their own twenty. But the final minutes of the game were anti-climactic. As he walked off the field with his teammates, dodging a swarming media and congratulating Dallas players juiced from their resounding victory, Beebe had no idea his rundown would long survive the confetti and predictable TV sound bites raining down on the Pasadena stadium.

Only later, in the somber locker room, did he get an inkling of what his fourth-quarter pursuit meant. Club owner and founder Ralph Wilson walked through the door. Strolling past his franchise quarterback and a trio of other future Hall-of-Famers, he made his way directly to the diminutive wide receiver who was sitting by himself, hunched over and head down. At first, Beebe only saw the owner's brown leather loafers that, despite his wealth and status, Wilson had purchased from a local department store. Then he felt the man's hand on his shoulder.

"Son, I'm mighty proud of what you did out there today," he said when Beebe raised his eyes. "We may have lost the game, but you exemplify what the Buffalo Bills are all about. Thank you for showing the world who we really are."

Beebe was caught off guard. And he was just as surprised when word came down he was requested for the post-game interview, even before Coach Marv Levy or Kelly got the call. The room full of sports reporters — from Scranton, Pennsylvania, to Seoul, Korea — wanted answers. The words were varied, but the question was the same: Why, they wanted to know, did he run eighty-two yards to tackle Leon Lett in a play that meant absolutely nothing to the game?

That Super Bowl moment would one day become among ESPN's top plays in NFL history, shown over and over again on highlight reels for years to come. It would earn Beebe the first ESPY ever handed out by the sports network as Play of the Year. It would also bring unwanted notoriety to Lett, who would be shunned by disgruntled fans and vilified, even threatened, by gamblers who lost thousands of dollars because he blew a touchdown that would have earned Dallas the most points ever scored in a Super Bowl.

But on that Sunday in Pasadena, Beebe could not figure out what all the fuss was about. Following Christ's message, he simply did what he had been taught in a series of life lessons – some harder than others – from the time he was a small boy throwing a football around in the backyard and dreaming of playing in Rose Bowl Stadium. Even when the odds are stacked against you, never give up.

Never. Ever.

CHAPTER 1 – Harnessing Young Talent

The moment he walked through the door, Barb Beebe knew that her son, his face painted in grimy sweat, was not in a good mood.

Tossing his foul, over-stuffed gym bag onto the kitchen floor, Don gave it a hard kick before heading to the cookie jar and grabbing a fistful of oatmeal bars. Upset or not, Don had a sixteen-year-old stomach that was impossible to keep full, a fact reflected in the Beebe family's ever-expanding grocery bill.

As much as she'd like to get new carpeting for their comfortable but unassuming ranch house, located in a comfortable but unassuming subdivision in tiny Sugar Grove, Illinois, Barb was practical. She realized expendable income would be limited while her rambunctious family was still in its growing stage.

"Rough practice?" Barb asked, already anticipating the affirmative grunt she got back from her son. "If it makes you feel any better, we're having pot roast tonight, and I peeled plenty of extra potatoes 'cause I figured you would be hungry."

Food, especially her pot roast, and yes, even the meatloaf, could always bring the Beebe men out of a funk. This time it didn't seem to help. Her eldest boy had something heavy on his mind and she wondered if she should just let it rest until his father could deal with it. But his dad, who worked nights as a meter reader for the gas company, wouldn't be home for a while. Besides, Donny made the decision for her.

"I'm quitting football after this year, Mom," he said as he plopped his slim but muscular five-foot-seven frame onto a wooden stool. He kicked off his sneakers and began rubbing his left shin that showed signs of a bruise in its early not-yet-ugly stage. "New injury?" asked Barb, who at this point was so used to sports wounds, even the sight of oozing blood did little to alarm her. Donny didn't seem to hear her. "Today we ran about thirty sprints and half the guys were just goofing off, so we had to run another ten and I thought I was gonna puke."

Barb watched her son in amazement as he wolfed down a couple of the icing-coated bars in mid-sentence. "Then, we ran a bunch of pass routes," Donny continued. "But so many kids kept messing up, Coach had us do it all again."

Barb opened the oven to check on the meat and potatoes. She figured it wasn't just the brutal practices that were responsible for her son's sour attitude. And she was right.

"None of that would matter if we could win a game or two," Don complained. "But c'mon, Ma, we got creamed by Plainfield last week, and you know the same thing's gonna happen on Friday with Sycamore. Our team stinks and half the guys don't even care if we get humiliated every time we go out on the field."

Barb had heard this lament before. Sugar Grove was one of four small Kane County towns, located on the far western ring of the Chicago area, that fed into the Kaneland School District. The scrappy Kaneland Knights usually played bigger schools, yet were competitive in most sports. But the last couple seasons had not been good for the football team. And one thing she knew about her kid: He did not like to lose.

This time, Donny was serious about hanging up his cleats for good. It broke her heart to see him losing interest in a game he'd played with such passion since the age of eight. Even early on, Donny harbored dreams a whole lot bigger than the fields he played on. And as proof, all she had to do was glance out her kitchen window to the backyard, its potential beauty marred with a patchwork lawn that would probably never recover from years of sneakers pounding away on its turf.

Almost every day during the summer and well into those spectacular fall weekends in Illinois, Donny would grab the battle-scarred football from the garage, then round up a group of kids — little brothers, cousins, neighbors, anyone he could coax or bribe into playing — and transform his backyard into the Rose Bowl. And he played with a fierce determination that would fascinate his parents as well as frustrate his playmates.

"How many times do we have to run this play?" his brother Danny, three years younger, would ask as sweat poured from his face. The answer was always the same: "Until we get it right."

Donny, the middle of five kids and oldest boy, most often was the quarterback. Sometimes he was the wide receiver or the running back. And when there weren't enough players for his impromptu games, he'd turn into a combination of all three.

"Watch his eyes," Don Beebe Sr. would tell his wife when the couple would take a few minutes from their hectic day to take in the backyard game. "See how they get darker? It's almost like they are burning."

His father recognized the competitive drive that fueled his eldest son. And Donny did not apologize for it. The fact was, he did not like to lose ... and not just in sports. When the family would travel the 520 miles to a resort in Remer, Minnesota, for their annual summer vacation, they held a fishing derby, with their dad keeping track of who caught the most fish by placing dots on a large piece of cardboard. If Donny wasn't in first place, he would forgo all other activities — card games, trips into town to bowl or get ice cream, even dinner — to stand on the dock with his fishing pole so he could regain the lead.

"Forget it," the older Don told his son at one point in the competition. "I'm not going to make 118 dots for all the bluegills you caught. I'll make one big dot to represent them all."

Barb smiled at the memory. In every aspect of his life, Donny set the bar high and would get into a funk if he did not reach it. And most of that intensity was directed toward the one thing he loved most — sports. When Donny was in second grade, while sitting with his Aunt Marian in the pews at Soul's Harbor Church at Sullivan and Randall roads in Aurora, the pastor called upon those in the congregation to come to the front of the altar and ask Jesus into their lives. Barb and Don Beebe were devout Christians who did more than make their lively brood go to church every Sunday morning. They used Scriptures to help their kids understand life's lessons, whether those lessons were as simple as learning to share with others or as complicated as understanding the unexpected death of a beloved family member.

Don and Barb didn't just talk the talk. Their commitment to Jesus Christ was unyielding. And like all his siblings, Donny seemed to grasp what a faith-centered world was all about. So he knew exactly what he was doing when he accompanied his aunt to the altar at age seven and told the pastor he was ready to take the Christian walk.

"Is there anything you want to ask God right now?" Marian whispered to her nephew after he had just accepted Jesus into his heart.
The youngster was quick to respond. "Yes, I would like to ask God if I can be something special in sports." And now, here he was, ready to give up football before even his high school career had a chance to take off.

Barb sighed. Her son was determined, but that also meant he was stubborn. And when he made his mind up about something, it often took a more strong-willed person to convince him he didn't always know what he was talking about.

That equally strong-willed person would be home in about 20 minutes. "Well, you've got two games left to play in this season, and you know it's not good to make any big decisions when you're upset," Barb told her disgruntled son as she began placing plates on the round oak table. "Go jump in the shower. You're a sweaty mess. After dinner you need to sit down with your father and talk to him about all this."

Barb didn't let her son know it, but she was concerned. She marveled at Donny's competitiveness, but she also realized that, like his stubbornness, it was as much a liability as an asset. Playing to win was one thing, but it wasn't everything. It wasn't even possible to come out on top every time. Life was full of losses; big ones, small ones. And how someone deals with those defeats can say a whole lot more about him than how he handles the victories. Her son, it seemed, was ready to give up when the going got tough. And life was going to get a whole lot tougher for him because, well, that's just the way God tends to write the scripts.

Barb had led this discussion with Donny and his siblings numerous times over the past few years. Every day can bring new hurdles. Sometimes you fly over them on your first attempt and don't look back as you prepare for the next one standing in your way. Sometimes you hit them hard, even take a nasty tumble, get a little bloodied and bruised. Then you get back up and go at it again.

Donny had heard plenty about hurdles already in his young life. But Barb wondered now if this kid had been listening as intently as he could have been. Two hours later, while she was finishing up the dishes, the lesson continued. Only there was no talk of hurdles. And the teacher, this time, wasn't quite as patient.

5

"There's no way any son of mine is going to quit in the middle of a season," said Don Sr., perched on the edge of the well-worn brown sofa and staring his kid straight in the eye. "And there will be no negotiations, so don't even bother trying."

Oblivious to the chatter going on around him at the table, Don had spent most of dinner rehearsing what he figured were some good point/counter points. But the tone of his father's voice told him there would be no room for debate tonight.

"OK, I'll finish out the season," he agreed. "But next year let me just concentrate on basketball. You know, Dad, how much I want to play sports in college. And if I put everything into basketball, then I can probably get a scholarship."

The elder Beebe had already figured out where his son's argument was headed. Only, he wasn't buying it. Donny was a gifted athlete. It didn't matter if he was playing football, baseball or basketball. But Don Sr. was a realist. The kid was sixteen and he probably wasn't going to grow a whole lot more. He certainly was never going to be tall enough to play college basketball. If Donny was really set on getting a scholarship, it was more than likely going to come from football.

That's because the one thing the kid had going for him, besides decent hands, was incredible speed. Not that his dad had ever timed him. Nor had the coaches, for that matter. But it was obvious from anyone who saw him run that the kid was a burner.

"Here's the deal, Donny," the elder Beebe began. "You can quit football on one condition: You do another fall sport in its place."

Donny's shoulders slumped. "C'mon Dad, that only leaves cross country. And that's not even a sport. It's just running – and more running."

"And all that running and more running will get you in great shape for basketball season," his father countered. "I'm going to leave the decision up to you, Donny. But I think you know what you need to do."

The teen muttered under his breath, his displeasure evident. But the following afternoon, Donny showed up for football practice. He didn't realize it until much later, but as good as his mom's pot roast had been that night, his dad's direction had been even better.

* * *

Kaneland would only boast one win Don's junior year. After losing the final game against Morris in a thrashing that saw him on the field a total of two-and-a-half minutes, the young athlete was again ready to hang up his cleats for good. His dad, Donny begrudgingly conceded, was probably right: Cross country would be good conditioning for basketball. And basketball was his first love, after all.

But a young Kaneland High history teacher had other ideas. Despite his stature, just five-foot-seven, Joe Thorgesen had been a star quarterback at West Aurora High School who went on to letter at Illinois Wesleyan. After earning his teaching degree, he joined the staff at Kaneland, a consolidated high school that took in students from four small towns and was surrounded by the corn and soybean fields of rural Kane County. Thorgesen soon became a favorite with students for his affable personality and genuine love for the kids. He could be hard-nosed and tough to please, but he was also quick to spot the potential in those who took his class or showed up on his playing field.

As the new sophomore coach during Donny's junior year, Thorgesen saw something special in the young Beebe who now, as a junior, was playing on the varsity team. Even more important than the speed in the athlete's legs was the fire in his heart. So when Thorgesen was promoted to head varsity coach Beebe's senior year, he knew exactly what he needed to do to turn Kaneland's dismal record around.

"We are going to harness this kid's talents," he told his staff. "And we're going to use that talent to win us some games." Later, he gave that same promise to Donny. "Son, give me a chance. I've seen you run and I've watched how you handle yourself with the other guys on the team. You're a born leader. Come out for the team, and I promise, you'll get the ball. I also promise we're going to start winning a game or two."

The Knights did better than that. Six games into the 1982 season, they were undefeated. One of Kaneland's most impressive upsets was over its rival, Morris High School, located 40 miles south on Route 47. The Redskins always seemed to field a much bigger, faster and meaner team, and the Knights had never beaten them in the history of the school. Not only did the smaller Kaneland squad keep from getting blown out the first half, two unlikely Morris fumbles in the fourth quarter put the underdogs within six points.

Then, with forty-eight seconds left in the game, Don threw a halfback pass — a beautiful thirty-two-yard spiral — to wide receiver Todd Gramly, who ran it effortlessly into the end zone. Kaneland's kicker had a strong leg, but he'd been struggling for much of the season. On this historic night, however, Kyle VanSickle earned hero status by booting the ball through the middle of the uprights for the win, turning the field into a black-and-white sea of screaming Knights students.

And yelling the loudest for the running back who had thrown the touchdown pass was a pretty Kaneland cheerleader named Diana Beckley.

CHAPTER 2- Falling Hard

Don couldn't clearly remember the first time he kissed Diana. But he had a good excuse for the memory lapse, considering it happened back in Mrs. Baker's second-grade classroom. He did recall Diana was cute, even then, with long blond curls and bangs hanging well past the tops of her large brown eyes. And when she planted one on him in the reading section at the back of the room, he kinda liked it – although he wasn't about to let his buddies Greg Kramer or Scott Sheridan think it was anything but gross.

Except for his two older sisters, Don didn't give girls much thought in grade school, or junior high for that matter. He was way too busy with more important things, like shooting hoops in the driveway. Or catching fly balls and hitting home runs at the Lions baseball diamond. Or throwing around the old football, which seemed to weather the years a whole lot better than the Beebes' backyard, despite his dad's attempts to keep some grass growing there.

By the time Donny got to high school, he was still aware of who Diana was. Not only was she the prettiest member of the J.V. cheerleading squad, during sophomore year she and Don were voted by the students to represent their class on Homecoming court. Diana had a date with some big-shot junior, and after intense pressure from his sisters and mom, Don had asked Sue Kayzar to the dance. She was a good friend, which meant he wouldn't be stumbling all over his words when he talked to her. No way was he into dressing up in a suit and tie and dancing close to a girl, but Sue helped him get rid of his jitters. By the time they called the Homecoming court to the dance floor, it seemed sort of natural when

Donny put his arm around Diana and they swayed awkwardly to Olivia Newton-John's "Hopelessly Devoted to You."

"You look really pretty," he offered, while praying those four words came off a lot smoother than he felt.   "Thanks, so do you … I mean, you look handsome … not pretty," Diana replied. And her laugh immediately set him at ease, at least long enough for him to finish the dance and gracefully exit the spotlight.

"It was OK," he told his buddies, who were waiting for him in the corner of the room, when the whole silly ceremony had concluded. "At least I didn't step on her toes."

Later that night he wasn't quite so blasé. "I got to dance with Diana Beckley and she's hot, hot, hot!" he practically yelled when ordered to give a full report to his mom and sisters.

Still, even in those first two years of high school, Don was too busy hanging out with his buddies to give much thought to the opposite sex. He and his brother Dan were always up to no good with barrel-chested Jeff Still and his lanky brother Jimmy. The Still boys, with their crew cuts, giant feet and even larger smiles, lived down the street. The two sets of siblings hung out so frequently, most folks in the neighborhood referred to them as the Four Musketeers. Sometimes their nicknames weren't quite as noble — like when they were hitting rocks with their bats into the neighbor's yard. Despite their impressive skills at the plate, mostly at the Lions Park baseball field, there were plenty of wayward stones flying all over the neighborhood. One Saturday, a good-sized rock got away from all of them — Jeff blamed Don; Don pointed the finger at Dan; Dan could have sworn it was Jimmy. But who the heck really knew anything – except that it went through Lynette Lambert's big shiny picture window.

All four were called on the carpet —in the Beebes' family room. Don Sr.'s frown revealed his displeasure as he shot a hard look at the line of grim-faced suspects. "It doesn't really matter whose bat it came off," he told the boys who were now staring intently at the tops of their dust-covered sneakers. "You're going to combine all your money equally and pay the bill to get that window repaired."

This neighborhood posse seemed to be in constant trouble. But truth be told, if they would have gotten nailed every time they were up to no good, they would have had to fork over their allowances, spending money earned from part-time jobs and maybe even their salaries through age thirty. One of their favorite games was "driveway dunking." As Don was delivering The Beacon- News in the afternoons, he and the crew-cut crew would ride through the neighborhood on bikes, stopping often enough to slam their basketballs as hard as they could through every net along the paper route. The goal was to use as much force as possible, and that often meant running a few steps up the side of the garage to gather enough steam for the big jam. The result was sometimes a torn net or a bent rim. And if a cop would have pulled up and asked them what they were up to, more than likely they would have asked him if he wanted to take a shot.

As his mom would lament to her husband after lights were out, "They're really good kids … they just don't know how to contain all that energy." Who's to say: The St. Charles Youth Detention Center just up the road on Route 38 could have been in their future had things continued in the same direction. But donning a Kaneland uniform was the goal of every kid who grew up in Sugar Grove, as well as the surrounding towns of Kaneville, Maple Park and Elburn. And all that energy suddenly became rerouted when the boys got involved in high school sports.

Other transformations were occurring, as well. Donny may not have been all that excited about the football team's chances in the Little Seven Conference that junior year, but he sure liked the fact the girls smiled sweetly at the jocks when they swaggered down the halls. Now here it was, just a few days before the first game against Yorkville, and during the school carnival he got word through a buddy who got it from another friend's girlfriend who got it from a supposedly very reliable source that Diana Beckley wanted to go out with him.

"You have to go over there and ask her out, Beebs," said his friend, Greg Kramer, who always carried a dare in his back pocket, along with a pack of gum and the week's current play sheet. "This is your big chance, and if you don't strike now you may not get the chance again."

One thing about Donny Beebe: He could never turn his back on a challenge. Even if he'd never had a real date with a girl — much less kissed one — he wasn't about to pass on something like this. Don finally summoned up the courage to approach Diana at the carnival's dunk tank, where she and the other cheerleaders were favorite targets for Illinois farm boys with out-of-control arms and libidos to match.

When Don sidled up to the tank, Diana shot him one of her easy smiles. "So how many times did you go in the water?" he asked.

"As of now, six times," she replied, laughing. "Doug Wise threw so wild he almost beaned me." She paused, squinting at Don through the bright sun. Maybe she was waiting for him to reply or ask another question. Maybe she was just trying to figure out why he'd come to chat with a person sitting in a dunk tank.

Donny mentally heaved a long sigh – then took the plunge. "So Diana, a group of us, we're going out for pizza in a little while, and I was wondering …would you like to go?"

12

"Well, sure. I mean, I'd like to come along," she said. "But I have to stay here until the carnival is over. Either that or find another cheerleader to take my place." Was there sincerity in her voice? It was hard to tell.

In the end, Diana couldn't find a sub, so Don wolfed down a sausage extra-cheese pizza with his buddies, who worked hard to reassure him she really did seem interested in going out with him. But Don wasn't feeling so confident. He may have been a three-sport athlete, but when it came to girls, he was pretty much a bench warmer. It had taken everything he had to ask Diana out for this stupid pizza he was now eating all by himself. "I'm not going to do it again," he told himself later that night as he played over the conversation in his mind. He had his break, and it didn't pan out.

In fact, it was a break in the alternator of Greg Kramer's Honda a few days later that drove, quite literally, Don and Diana together. The guys, on their way to football practice, stopped to pick up Frank Kigyos, when the car sputtered pathetically and refused to start. Knowing how loud Coach Thorgesen yelled when anyone was even a few minutes late to practice, the boys sprinted to Frank's house in the subdivision, only to find out he'd already left for practice.

"Hey, doesn't Diana Beckley live nearby?" asked Greg, who took perverse pleasure in teasing Don incessantly about the pretty blond cheerleader these past twenty-four hours. "If she knows Donny-boy needs a ride, I'll bet she'll drop everything she's doing and take us to practice."

Don had no desire to see if his friend was right, but desperate times called for desperate measures. He led the way to Diana's house and rang the bell, trying to pretend this was just another door on his paper route.

Her mother answered, and Don held his breath after asking if Diana was home. As it turned out, she was heading to the school herself to turn in the money from the dunk tank. When the football players piled into the cheerleader's baby blue Duster, his teammates almost fell over each other scrambling into the back seat; leaving Don sitting up front with their impromptu chauffeur. After arriving at the football field, the back cleared even more rapidly. "Too bad they can't move that fast on a football field," Don cracked.

When Diana laughed, his heart did that same little fluttery thing he had noticed at the homecoming dance. Should he? Was he crazy to try again? Hey, no pain, no gain. Isn't that what the coaches always preached?

"So, I was wondering, Diana, if you would like to go to a show with me on Saturday and then maybe we could grab something to eat. I mean, if you're busy or something we could do it another ..."

"I think that would be fun," she mercifully broke in. "Call me tonight and we can figure out the plans."

Practice that day was harder than usual, especially with the late August heat beating down on the Kaneland squad. The first game was in four days. He was pumped about his first date, for sure. But Don was focused on a different goal as he eyed the senior running back who was his competition for the starting position. Diana Beckley was special, but no girl was coming between him and his goals. And he told her as much that Saturday night. After picking up his date in the family's white station wagon, the couple went to see a really bad 3-D movie at the Tivoli Theater, then grabbed a bite to eat.

"When I was seven and gave myself to the Lord, I asked him to help me do something special in sports. I just feel a real draw in that direction," he said as they sat next to each other in a booth at Pizza Hut, finally sharing that extra-cheese pie, this time a large pepperoni with green peppers.

Conversation that evening revolved around a diversity of topics: They chatted about school, family, friends. And to Diana's surprise, much of their three-hour dinner was about his relationship with Jesus Christ. Diana was intrigued. She'd never gone out with a guy who was this intense – or so deeply involved in his faith.

"I could never date anyone seriously who did not feel that same commitment," he stated matter-of-factly. "It's just too important to me."

Even as he said those words, Don knew this girl – no matter how great she seemed – didn't fall into that category yet. What he didn't know was that in two weeks, Diana would be saved at a youth rally at First Assembly of God Church on Galena Boulevard. Still, by the end of that night, when he planted a doorstep kiss on her cheek — five minutes before her father's deadline of 11 p.m. — he was convinced she'd be in his life for many years.

For the first time in his memory, Donny fell asleep thinking about something other than sports. It was a weird feeling — but totally, incredibly amazing.

CHAPTER 3 – Swallowing Pride

Despite the lessons that had been drilled into him by his parents and high school coaches about all those hurdles that needed to be cleared, Donny Beebe was ready to call it quits again.

But first, he had to puke.

Coach R. Bruce Craddock, a Marine captain in Vietnam and now in his first year as head coach of the Western Illinois University Leathernecks, had been none too pleased with the three-hour workout his team had just completed. So he made them run — wearing pads and helmets in the ninety-degree heat — for another two miles.

"If you sorry wannabes think you know what it takes to survive this program, I suggest you stop using your pea brains and start using those sorry butts of yours," he screamed, as the team started yet another slog around the parameters of Western's athletic compound. "You mama's boys are moving so slow you couldn't catch a fart in a windstorm!"

This day's grueling workout, punctuated every few seconds with Crad's staccato orders, was not unique. Since arriving on the WIU campus here in Macomb, Illinois, two weeks earlier for football camp, Beebe had quickly realized playing in high school was like a backyard pickup game compared to college ball.

Not that he hadn't been jacked about the opportunity. After a standout senior year in football, including All-Conference and All-Area honors, Beebe traded his cleats for a pair of basketball shoes that earned him a few more plaques for his bedroom wall. Then, just for kicks and because speed really was his thing, that spring, the five-foot-ten sprinter, after getting disqualified for a false start in the hundred, hauled in a second-place medal in the two hundred at the Illinois state track meet.

Life was good for that little kid who asked God to help him do something special in sports. But as proud as he was of his Kaneland accomplishments, Beebe had his goals set a whole lot higher. Problem was, the MVP hardware and write-ups in the local sports pages didn't bring out a barrage of scouts or coaches offering him a clear path toward those goals. Beebe was fast, no doubt about it. He could make the big plays, and his intensity and die-hard mentality on a field, track or court demonstrated his leadership. But Donny was physically too small by NCAA standards to garner much attention from those who counted most. There just weren't too many Division I schools interested in a short white running back, even if they could figure out which country roads would lead them to Kaneland High School.

Western Illinois was the exception. Coach Craddock's offer from this state school of twelve thousand students was the full ride Don Sr. was hoping for. Even though WIU didn't play with the big boys of Division I-A, its Division I-AA status wasn't anything to sneeze at. Western Illinois went up against perennial Gateway Conference powerhouses like Northern Iowa and Southern Illinois. And the Leathernecks had managed to propel plenty of All-Conference stars into the NFL, including Patriots fullback Larry Garron, Bills defensive back Booker Edgerson, 49es defensive back Jim Jackson and Patriots defensive tackle Dave Tipton.

There was a reason the Leathernecks, always big and strong, were the only nonmilitary institution in the nation with permission to use the Marine Corps logo and bulldog mascot. And Craddock looked every bit the part of a Leatherneck: Six-foot-two and tipping the 250-pound mark, Coach Crad wore his shirts tight and his hair crewed.

It's no wonder he ran his football program more like a boot camp. Kids were too pampered, he growled to his staff, his team, and even the parents who brought their sons on those high-pressure recruiting visits. His job, if he wanted to turn out a competitive program, was to teach fledgling prima donnas that "football is war."

"The only way to win the battle is to work harder and smarter than your enemy," Crad would bellow to those who dared question his intensity. Only, Don didn't know if he was going to survive long enough to go into battle.

On the first day of practice, Craddock ordered the team to run twenty-four wind sprints. Beebe started out like gangbusters in those first ten, easily crossing the finish line first. But the rookie, clueless about collegiate football programs, gave it his all too quickly, and found himself bringing up the rear in the final sets. That didn't endear the speedster to his coach one little bit. After yelling obscenities at Don – with the more tame referring to Beebe as an old lady wearing support hose – he ordered all tailbacks into the crouching position off the line of scrimmage.

"Spread those legs wide! Get those lazy butts down! Lower! Lower!" he barked.

Five minutes into the crouch, Don could feel the quiver. After ten minutes, the legs began to shake. Another five added on, and he felt like his lower half was being bombarded with Fourth of July sparklers. After twenty minutes, Crad strolled past the tailbacks, his movements slow and deliberate as he inspected their stances. Don saw Crad's Marine-issue boots come to a halt behind him. He heard a slow, low growl. Beebe squeezed his eyes shut and held his breath.

Suddenly, Crad kicked Beebe in the posterior with the force of a grenade launcher. It sent the surprised athlete sprawling.

18

"I told you, BUTT DOWN!" the Marine screamed.

* * *

Don still felt the emotional sting from that first day of practice now, almost two weeks later as he and his teammates pounded out those extra two miles. All around him, he could hear the desperate panting of his buddies falling behind as the sun beat down on them. For the past mile, Don had tried to fight off a cramp. Now the pain was an electric jolt radiating up his left thigh. He stared at the ground and tried to imagine a cool spray of water running over his face and seeping into his parched throat.

His prayer at that moment was simply for the chance to see another sunrise. "I know I ask for a lot from you, Lord," he begged silently as he forced one foot in front of the other. "But please don't let this crazy man kill me."

Craddock didn't just shout out orders and expect the team to follow. He ran alongside the young men in black and purple, belting out Marine songs as the parade of Leathernecks labored toward their intended goal. Nothing summed up Craddock's coaching style more than when the team finally made it to their destination, the archery course. There stood a large round, red-and-white target, complete with purple bull's-eye. But instead of stopping the team and turning around, Crad – minus even a hat, much less a helmet – ran head first into the middle of the target.

"Is he stark raving crazy?" Beebe heard a player shout from behind him as Craddock bounced off the target and stumbled backward.

Seemingly unfazed by the gaping cut now in the middle of his head, the head coach stared at the target for a moment, cursed, then charged it again, ramming his head into the center for a second time. The barrage of four-letter words that erupted from his mouth surprised even these seasoned Craddock players, some of whom shifted uncomfortably as the litany of cuss words continued.

"Blasted!" he finally shouted, holding his big hand to his head that began gushing blood from the three-inch cut. "Now I have to go and get some stitches in this thing. And that means I'll be late for dinner and my wife ain't gonna like that one bit."

Beebe had never seen anything like it. He and the other players stared at their wounded coach in silence, too afraid to speak, much less laugh – and grateful for the unexpected break they received, thanks to Coach's surprising run-in with the bull's-eye. That respite was short-lived. Forty-five minutes later, back at the practice field to the east of Hanson Field, the team hunkered around Crad, begging for mercy with their glassy eyes. Coach, obviously deciding stitches were overrated as he continued to ooze blood, was still not happy. He made them run again, this time across campus and into a wide-open hayfield.

"Circle the wagons! Circle the wagons!" he barked. The delirious squad fell into position. "Now drop and give me twenty up-downs!" Crad ordered in a bark that was more like a rabid dog than a college coach. "And I don't want to hear one word of whining."

The team obeyed. But they weren't quick enough, so those twenty turned into another twenty and another twenty and another twenty and another twenty …

The first to bite the dust was big Keith Blue, a three-hundred-pound lineman with a heart as big as his XXL helmet. On count ninety-two, Blue went down on his knees and started throwing up what remained of his early morning breakfast. Beebe almost lost the contents of his own stomach looking at his teammate's regurgitated scrambled eggs and what appeared at first glance as catsup.

"Medic!" Crad yelled. "We need a medic over here now. NOW!"

"Sir, do you mean a trainer?" asked Bryan Cox, the former All-State linebacker from East St. Louis High School and future NFL pro.

"Yeah, sure, a trainer. A medic, whatever," the coach glared. "Move out of the way and let's get this boy some water."

Next to give up his breakfast was Steve Wisniewski, who made some weird sort of sobbing noise as he hung his head and barfed on the dry, wilted weeds around him.

Beebe knew if he puked, nothing would come up. In the weeks since football camp began, he'd barely been able to eat, and what he did manage to keep down usually came out the other end in the bathroom. He would sometimes lie in bed at night wondering if this is how it feels to die. He entered camp weighing only 165 pounds, but already Crad had sliced off twenty more – and showed no signs of letting up.

Don was eighteen years old and absolutely miserable being away from Sugar Grove. Yes, he missed Mom and Dad and the rest of the family, but he and Diana had something special going. He was certain this was the woman he would marry — and the two-hour phone calls every night just weren't a substitute for being with her.

But he was more than homesick or lovesick. "I can't do this anymore, Di," he confessed later that night. "I'm running a temperature again, and I can't stop shaking. I'm really afraid I'm going to end up in the hospital if I stay here much longer."

Diana had felt his desperation growing over the past few days. "Call your parents," she suggested. "You need to let them know just how bad it is."

Barb was sympathetic: His father was not. "Son, you've got an opportunity most kids would give their eye teeth for," he reminded Donny.

"Sorry, Dad, this time I really don't think I have a choice," the younger Beebe replied, swallowing his pride and choking on its bitter aftertaste.

Two days later, Don returned home, discouraged yet still convinced God's road for him led to a future in sports.

Only, he didn't have a clue how to get back on it.

CHAPTER 4 – Losing Focus

Diana finished her phone conversation and did something quite out of the ordinary. She slammed down the receiver. Hard.

Her mom heard it. Her sisters Brenda and Teresa heard it. All three looked at each other, eyebrows raised but mouths closed. Frustrations were mounting and, knowing Di's personality, they were pretty sure things were not going to stay status quo for long. "Sorry," she murmured as tears filled her eyes. "But darn it, I've had it with him!"

Ann Beckley knew better than to go after Diana as the emotional teen marched into her bedroom, banging the door behind her. When Don called a half hour later, she was surprised her daughter agreed to take the call. Diana sighed as she accepted the phone. "What do you want?" she asked her boyfriend of four years.

That seemed to be the million-dollar question these days. It had been a rough year or so for the young couple. After returning home from Western Illinois University twenty pounds lighter and emotionally weaker, Don knew he had to figure out his next move. He'd gotten himself into this position, and he was the only one who could get out of it. One thing for sure, though: Thanks to Coach Craddock, Beebe had no desire to set foot on a football field any time soon. That didn't mean he was giving up his dream of playing college sports.

"So, what about basketball?" suggested his dad, trying to show as much support as he could muster after Don relinquished his scholarship at Western. "I don't think you're going to be happy if you're not playing somewhere."

Don had decided the same thing on that long ride home from WIU. Days after returning to Sugar Grove, he enrolled at Aurora College, a private D-III school just minutes from home. Beebe had been a star basketball player in high school, so the Spartans accepted him enthusiastically when he asked to join the team. It didn't take long for him to impress the coaches with his die-hard hustle and amazing vertical leap. For a while, it seemed Don was exactly where he wanted to be: playing his favorite sport on a team that was close to home, family and girlfriend.

The Spartans were a friendly group of athletes who accepted the walk-on into the fold immediately. And Don thrived on the competitiveness. But unlike most of his teammates and students in his classes, Don was in school for all the wrong reasons. He wasn't a drinker so it wasn't like he was in to the party scene. But he wasn't into the books, either, since he had no idea what direction his life was heading. With little or no enthusiasm for any of his classes, Don began skipping more than he attended. That didn't set well with Diana, who was working full-time as a secretary at State Farm Insurance and looking forward to the day she and Don would start a future together. Only, right now she wasn't seeing a whole lot of future. There were times she felt as if she didn't even know the undisciplined young man whose eyes had once burned with such focus. It was a change that was not only surprising, it was downright disturbing.

No question, Donny needed time to figure everything out. But he sure wasn't going to get there by hanging out with his buddies, which was all he wanted to do now. If he wasn't practicing or traveling with the team, he was part of a pickup game of basketball; or impromptu round of golf; or any other athletic contest the guys could concoct in a moment's notice.

"At some point, you have to put me above sports," Diana told Don one day after yet another week without contact except for late-night phone conversations. "Right now, your priorities are all out of whack, and that's not good for anybody; not you, not me, and certainly not us."

24

No question Don was drifting. Once basketball season was over, the high-octane drive he'd always displayed had shifted to low gear. Unsure about what he was supposed to do next, Beebe knew Diana was right. He had to refocus. But on what?

The answer seemed to appear when his brother-in-law offered him a full-time job with his family's siding business. Beebe dropped out of school and joined the blue-collar work force. It was a great way to make some decent money, and he certainly didn't mind the physical labor or the long hours outdoors.

But that was two years ago, and the only change Diana saw in Don's life was even more hours hanging out with the guys, now that he wasn't in school.

In truth, Diana never thought she'd be at this point. From the time they were in high school, she and Don had shared a closeness that was envied by everyone they knew. They were best friends as well as soul mates. So why did it seem that lately, she had to battle for any sort of attention from him?

On this night, she and Donny had made plans again to go to a movie. And once again, he had called to cancel because he'd just gotten home from work. Only she didn't believe him, not for one stupid minute. Yes, he did arrive home late. And yes, he had put in a long day. But Don had fallen into the habit of meeting his buddies at the gym, and what had started as a once a week basketball game had grown into a daily event — including this Friday evening.

When he finally called, it was well past eight o'clock. After a sweaty game of three-on-three, Don still had to take a shower, get dressed … and well, could he and Diana just do the movie the next night? Cancelling the date had been the last straw. And now, after she'd slammed the receiver down, here he was, trying awfully hard to make amends. Only she wasn't in a forgiving mood.

"I think we need to break up, Don," she said matter-of-factly. "I've been doing a lot of thinking about all this. I'm just tired of always being third in your life. Or fourth. Or wherever it is I happen to fall on any particular day."

"What the heck are you talking ..." he began. Diana was in no mood for a debate. "We'd made plans all week to go to this movie," she interrupted, the words that had rolled around in her mind for weeks now tumbling from her lips. "Yet you couldn't even get home in time for us to have a nice night out. I'm done, Donny. I'm sorry, but I've really had as much as I can take. I really do think we need to just call it quits. I'm tired of all this, and obviously you don't really care."

Her words caught Don by surprise. Diana couldn't actually mean what she was saying, could she? For crying out loud, they'd been together since their junior year. They had talked about getting married, buying a house. They had even discussed names for their future kids. Now, here she was, telling him to take a flying leap?

"Geeze, Di," he blurted, "that's the stupidest thing I've ever heard you say. You're blowing this thing way out of proportion. And what are you talking about, breaking up? We can't break up ... you're my best friend."

"Best friends respect each other, Don," she replied icily. "Best friends put the other person first. Best friends don't just think of themselves all the time. And you shouldn't be so surprised. We've talked over and over about how you spend too much time with your friends. You just didn't think I was serious. Now you know. But darn it, Donny, it's too late."

26

Too late? What the heck was that supposed to mean? Don felt panic rising in his throat. "But I love you, Diana," he choked out. "You gotta know that."

This time, before she hung up the phone, she whispered goodbye. With a lump the size of Texas gripping his gut, Don dialed Diana's number. No answer. He went into the garage, grabbed a ball and began hurling it against the outside wall. The thumping noise drew his brothers, who took one look at Don's face and disappeared back into the house. An hour later, he dialed Diana's number again. "Sorry, Don," her mother offered kindly. "She doesn't want to talk right now."

He tried again the next day, and the next day. Still, she ignored him. The following month was perhaps the worst in his life — even more horrific than when Craddock was beating the stuffing out of him. Don may have been sicker than a dog, but at least he had Diana to talk to every night. And he always had her beautiful face in his mind.

Oh, she was still constantly in his thoughts — every single minute of every single day. When he was up at five in the morning, throwing on his jeans and work boots for another day hanging siding, he thought of her. All day long, while he was hammering nails, he thought of her. At night, he would lie in bed and stare at the ceiling, convinced that her face was gazing back at him. Images of her seemed etched in his brain cells because now, he could no longer see her for real.

Well, that wasn't entirely true. He did see her ... dating one of his buddies who'd always had a crush on Diana. Don had to pray pretty hard on that one. He felt like going over to that traitor's house and kicking the snot out of him. But he also knew such antics would do little to endear him to the girl he wanted so desperately to win back. Nor did he feel like getting arrested.

It's not like he could get any sympathy from his own family. They all took Diana's side. "If you want her back," Barb told her despondent son, "then you need to show her you've changed."

"How can I show her I've changed," he moaned, "if she won't even talk to me?" Don was miserable. And he made everyone else just as miserable. It took all his energy to pull himself out of bed in the morning for work. And when he returned home, he did nothing but lie on the sofa watching TV and sulking. Or, for a change of pace, he'd stretch out across his bed and sulk.

Barb noticed the irony in her son's situation. "At least go out with your buddies," she suggested, her maternal patience wearing thin. "For heaven's sake, Don, you can't just hibernate for the rest of your life."

No, but he could keep pretty darn close tabs on Diana. On many occasions he'd find himself driving past her house, looking at her bedroom window and wondering if she was home, then getting sick to his stomach if she wasn't. Or he'd go past the State Farm office where she worked, and fantasize about making an appointment to see her. Maybe there was such a thing as insurance against a broken heart, he thought unhappily.

And yes, he also called her number. Twice. Both times he hung up, afraid to face her rejection again. His friends, bewildered but sympathetic to the changes they saw in Donny, tried to offer a branch of hope. "Just give it some time, man," Jeff Still told him when he grew tired of listening to his buddy's thirty-minute litany of why he and Diana belonged together. "If it's meant to be, it'll all work out."

But Don was never all that good at the patience thing. "I really need to talk to her again," he told his sister Beth, exactly thirty-six days after their breakup. "Just ask Diana if she'll meet me tonight. I promise it will be no more than half an hour."

The couple met at one of their favorite hangouts, Colonial Café on Galena Boulevard in Aurora. Don ordered a Kitchen Sink, the restaurant's gargantuan ice cream special that featured seven scoops of ice cream with five toppings. Usually, he would play with the gooey dish, swirling hot fudge, caramel, whipped cream and crunchy almonds around and around the edge of his spoon before stuffing that first bite into his mouth. Tonight he only stared unhappily at the dish, while Diana picked at her butterscotch sundae.

"Thanks for seeing me," he finally began his much-rehearsed apology. "You probably have figured out by now, I've been miserable this past month." She remained silent.

"I've done a lot of thinking, too." Don continued. "I hate being away from you. I mean, I really hate it. And even if you don't believe me, I just want you to know I'll never take you for granted again."

Diana lowered her head as she felt tears fill her eyes. When she lifted her hand to wipe them away, she hit the spoon perched in the sundae dish, and sent it sailing into the air, spitting ice cream and syrup all over her blouse before it finally landed on the floor.

Diana giggled, Don smiled, breaking the tension between them. "I missed you, too," she said.

With nothing but melting desserts between them, the couple sat at the table for three hours, with Don doing most of the talking. "I've done a lot of praying, a lot of soul-searching. Give me a year, Diana. I'll keep working for the siding company for no more than a year. And by that time, I promise, I'll have figured out what I need to do next."

Diana grabbed his hands and squeezed tightly. "I believe you, Don. My dad always told us that sometimes you have to hit the ground hard before you can climb back up again."

Truer words, Don would soon learn, had never been uttered.

CHAPTER 5 – Hanging Around

Don awoke in darkness and, like clockwork, reached to his left to silence the shrieking alarm. 4:45 a.m. He groaned, closed his eyes for a brief moment and wished for the 100th time in the last 100 days that he was doing something else with his life.

After more than two years helping his brother-in-law hang aluminum siding, rising before sunrise when the rest of the household slumbered, he should have been used to the drill by now. But it was one thing to greet the morning with a brilliant sunrise and warm temperatures. This was January of 1986 and the weatherman was rarely his friend these days.

Don couldn't remember what the exact high was supposed to be. But he recalled vividly the wind chill. Three below. With afternoon cloudiness bringing a 20 percent chance of snow flurries.

For a brief moment Don thought about crawling back under the covers and pretending that tightness still tickling the back of his throat was bad enough to call in sick. Although McQuade Siding and its current crew of two had only missed a week or so of work so far because of nasty weather, Chicago winters were still brutal for construction workers.

For some unfathomable reason, Bob McQuade loved the cold as much as Don hated it. But he knew he couldn't leave his brother-in-law high and dry today: If he didn't show up, Bob couldn't work either. And even in mid-winter, business was good, especially with all the new construction going on near the Naperville/Aurora border. The money was decent, too. Don had not only managed to toss a few thousand dollars in savings, he'd also laid down some serious cash for a drop-dead gorgeous 1983 black Cutlass Supreme.

But hanging siding wasn't even close to where he wanted to be at this time in his life. And he wasn't looking forward to chipping the ice off his windshield before heading over to his boss's house.

No need to think depressing thoughts on an already depressing day, he figured, as he flipped on the light just long enough to pull out a clean pair of long underwear. He took a whiff of the Levis he'd worn yesterday. Still good.

He stepped into the jeans and threw on a couple layers of shirts. He donned two pair of wool socks before lacing up his dirt-crusted work boots that were supposed to be left by the back door every night, orders of his mom. Only, she wasn't stirring; nor was anyone else, as he rummaged around in the kitchen for the makings of a brown bag lunch. No turkey, no cheese. Salami and a couple leafs of lettuce would have to suffice.

Don tossed the sandwich into the paper bag, along with some stale chips and the slightly-withered last apple in the vegetable drawer. Even if Bob wanted to try that new hamburger place around the corner from the job site, Don figured he could eat this meager lunch as a mid-morning snack. Cutting aluminum and hanging it three stories high wasn't exactly child's play, and he could work up a pretty sizable appetite by 10 o'clock, especially when breakfast was consumed before the first light of day.

Beebe listened to Jonathon Brandmeir on Chicago's WLUP as he drove the 10-minute ride to Bob's house. He honked the horn and his brother-in-law quickly appeared, bundled in similar layers and carrying the obligatory large silver thermos. Don parked the Cutlass, and the two men climbed into the cab of Bob's brown Datsun pickup with the white MCQUADE SIDING signage splayed across the covered bed.

The sun was beginning to make its morning debut. Sometimes he and Bob would pick up more supplies en route to the job site at the ever-expanding Brookdale subdivision. But today there was only one stop; at the Seven/Eleven on Route 59, where both men grabbed Big Gulp coffees and Bob bought his usual turkey and ham sandwich. After hesitating only a moment, Don purchased one, too – along with two donuts, a chocolate milk and banana that he consumed before the men even arrived at the two-story house on Reader Street.

Two hours later, Don was glad he'd bought the extra sandwich. He'd been working the band saw all morning, trimming the 12-foot strips of aluminum siding and trying not to notice the cold that was already nipping at his gloved hands, along with the ever-so-subtle bite of the saw's metal edges.

Luckily, the wind had not picked up much, which was even more a blessing to Bob, perched on the staging two stories up and pounding nails with a rhythm that kept perfect beat to Journey's "Only the Young" now playing on the truck's radio.

Despite the thermal he'd piled on that morning, Don was miserable. All this layering could only do so much to ward off this viscous January assault. At 10 o'clock he and Bob took a break and built a small fire with some of the construction remnants. Huddled around the welcoming flame, they used the music from the radio as background to what inevitably became their daily debates. No matter what time of year, no matter what else was going on, the conversations always centered on sports.

Today the discussion started with Michael Jordan's foot injury earlier in the Bulls season and whether his anticipated return after the broken bone healed would be in time to turn around the season. But this was the winter of 1986, and the conversation here, as in most offices, bars and family rooms in Chicagoland, quickly moved to Mike Ditka's near-perfect season his Bears were experiencing. The NFC Championship game was this Sunday, and there were few fans out there who didn't believe the magic was going to continue all the way through Super Bowl Sunday.

But who was to thank for this incredible season made for some interesting debates. Was it Ditka and his irreverent quarterback Jim McMahon, coupled with the incomparable Walter Payton at running back? Or were the real stars of the team on the other side of the ball under defensive coordinator Buddy Ryan? Both coaches – bombastic and media-savvy – were butting heads more often and the tension was mounting, along with those oftentimes lop-sided wins.

"Are you kidding me? Ryan deserves all the credit he's trying to get," argued McQuade. "His defense is the best the game's seen because he knows how to get the most out of each one of 'em. And I can guarantee you Dan Hampton, Mike Singletary and Richard Dent are future Hall of Famers. No way would we be here without 'em."

"I'm not saying Ryan's defense isn't good, man … But how can you discount the offense when you've got the fastest guy in the league right now, and the greatest running back of all time," Don countered, referring to Willie Galt and Payton. "Sure, defense wins championships, but you still gotta put points on the board. And these guys are putting lots of them up."

Bob wasn't convinced. "Payton's a legend, and I hope like heck we get to the Super Bowl so he can get at least one touchdown. No one deserves it more than him. But Galt, I don't know. He's fast. Just don't make him run more than a straight line or he gets caught up in his own jock strap. And even you have to agree McMahon is fun to watch but he's no Hall of Famer."

The friendly debate continued through two cups of lukewarm coffee. "Time to get back to the salt mines, bro," Bob reluctantly announced as he downed that last gulp. "Wanna go up on the ladder after lunch? We've got another five hours before we finish up here, and I wouldn't mind trading places for a few of those ...it's dang cold up there."

Don glanced up at the staging that stretched 15 feet in the air across the top of the newly-constructed home. He nodded to Bob, but inwardly groaned. His already miserable day just took a dramatic turn for the worse: As much as he disliked winter, Don hated heights even more.

That's why, as a kid, when his buddies were scampering up the sides of those big old oaks in the neighborhood, he'd volunteer to bring up the rear. And if they challenged him to climb higher, he would do so with his eyes half-closed and his heart in his throat.

Don, of course, was never one to turn down a dare. So he'd make the slow and steady climb, willing himself to another place, forcing his mind to think of Mom's meatballs and spaghetti or a spiraling football sailing across an open field. Then he would pray as hard as he'd ever prayed that he wouldn't tumble out of the tree, hitting branch after branch on his way down; and ending up splattered like a sack of ripe red tomatoes on the cold hard ground below.

His fear, he decided was not necessarily irrational. Or at least that's what he told himself. When Don was nine years old and walking on a path by the lake on a family vacation, he'd slipped on the loose dirt. Quick reflexes made it possible to grab on to a tree branch hanging near the steep embankment. And hang on he did ... for dear life. At least that's how it felt at the time, especially after making the mistake of looking down into the ravine below. But his dad, walking 20 yards in front, quickly came to the rescue, grabbing Don's hand and easily pulling him to safety.

Don figured, in hindsight, he'd never been in quite the peril he remembered. Mostly, he'd frozen. And later he had nightmares that he was falling through space, helpless and hopeless, only to awaken drenched in sweat. Unfortunately, his anxiety level didn't decrease as his age increased.

Man was not meant to go any higher than the top of a backyard fence, Don was convinced. Especially this man. No matter how aimlessly he seemed to be floating through life right now, he had no plans whatsoever to become a mountain climber, a jet pilot or a high-rise window washer in downtown Chicago.

Of course he hadn't planned on hanging aluminum siding, either. It's not like he didn't appreciate the chance to make some good money. The "hang guy" in the business was always the pro, with the sidekick working below on the saw. But from the beginning, Bob had begun teaching his brother-in-law the fine art of attaching those 12-foot strips to the sides of houses.

"I need you to learn this part of it," he'd said when Don confessed his dislike of heights. "The more you do it, the easier it will get. And if you're gonna work in this profession, you need to be able to nail the stuff to the sides of houses. Besides, I gotta have you up there sometimes so I can take breaks."

No one could ever accuse Don Beebe of not being a team player. But he never got used to going up the ladder, especially after taking a few tumbles through the years. None of the falls had caused any serious damage, except to his ego. But he figured it was just a matter of time before he broke a bone or cracked a rib or a whole lot worse.

"Sure, Bob," he replied, confident he was not showing the lack of confidence he really felt. "Since I'm already frozen solid, can't be much worse up there. Just keep the music in the truck going and the fire burning."

After prolonging lunch as long as he could — hard to do with the skimpy brown bag he brought today — Don climbed the ladder, approaching the chore like he did any challenge in life. It became a game. In this contest, the battle was between iron will and irrational fear. To win the game he had to make his mind go somewhere else. Today, as Bob cranked up the radio and REO Speedwagon, Don's thoughts went from Michael Jordan's likely comeback to another favorite topic: Diana

She was still working at the insurance company just a couple miles from the new subdivision, so she and Don tried to get together at least once a week for lunch. Since their near breakup, he'd tried really hard to spend more time with Diana. But after work each night, he still managed to get over to LaBeau's Fitness Center to play a little basketball with a group of guys. Diana still wasn't thrilled he spent so much time at the center, but at least she now understood how important it was he work up a sweat that didn't revolve around pounding penny-nails. Besides, he really was making time to see her more. And even though they hadn't talked about any wedding plans, both knew it was just a matter of time before they got engaged.

"You really need to have a better idea where you want to go with your life, honey," she had told him last night after he had gone over to her house for dinner. "Mom and Dad know we're getting married, but they want us to have a better plan in place ..."

No kidding, he thought. Bob and he made a great team. He knew his brother-in-law appreciated his friendship and work ethic. And Don really did love the manual labor. But in the end, he still was a reluctant construction worker, making ten bucks an hour cutting and nailing aluminum siding. Not much of a future when you're just hanging around.

* * *

Three days later, things didn't look that much rosier for the Los Angeles Rams as they huddled in the incredible cold while going down in in defeat at Soldier Field. Slouched on the sofa on this Sunday afternoon, half-sinking into the cushions flattened by years of brotherly horseplay, Don should have been nothing but pumped.

Watching the Bears during the NFL season was as much a part of the Beebe Sunday tradition as pancakes and early-morning church. This past year had been particularly amazing as the team had bulldozed its way to a near perfect – that lousy Miami Dolphins game, everyone agreed, was a total anomaly – 1985 season. And now, with just a couple minutes remaining in the fourth quarter, it looked like the Monsters of the Midway were well on their way to the Super Bowl. QB Jim McMahon had scored on a 16-yard run in the first quarter of the NFC Championship game; and struck again with a 22-yard pass to Willie Gault in the third quarter. Then, Kevin Butler kicked a 34-yard field goal in the first period, which was followed by a forced fumble, thanks to Richard Dent. That allowed linebacker Wilber Marshall to scoop up the ball and trot it into the end zone for a 52-yard touchdown.

Don's family hooped and hollered through the entire game as more chips and popcorn fell between the cushions of the couch. Don joined in, too, but his high-fives and cheers masked the black cloud gradually descending over him.

Despite the fiasco at Western Illinois, he still wanted to play football. And watching the athletes on TV, many of them close to his age, only reminded him of how far off track his dreams had gotten.

Don didn't think of himself as a moody person. At least he tried not to be. He knew how blessed he was to have the family and friends he had … not to mention such an amazing girlfriend. He knew plenty other people who struggled with physical and mental problems. And he felt especially fortunate to have such a deep faith that centered his life, no matter how often he got derailed. But there was something about watching those Sunday afternoon games …

When he was younger, Don and his buddies would grab the football after the Bears games were over and head outside for a little four on four – or even some seven on seven, depending on how many bodies showed up. Despite his love for the hometown team, he'd pretend to play for the San Diego Chargers – he liked the blue and gold uniforms. But Don wasn't a kid anymore. He was a grown man completely adrift. And here he was, sitting on the couch in the house he still lived in with his parents, watching others excel at a sport he loved. Then, tomorrow morning he'd wake up in the dark, turn off his alarm clock and climb out of bed so he could spend the next eight hours hanging siding in the freezing cold.

With the sounds of a Chicago victory still permeating the room, Don sunk into the couch even further as the post-game show began. His dad, noticing how quiet his oldest son was, tapped him on the shoulder.

"You OK, Donny," he asked. "The Bears are going to the Super Bowl and you look like you just lost your best friend."

Don stared straight ahead. "I'm fine, Dad. Just thinking."

Don Sr. knew his son well. The kid was a competitor. Always was. Always would be. And right now he wasn't competing, plain and simple. He sat down next to the young man and put his arm around Donny's shoulder. "I know you want to be playing. But you need to remember God has a plan for you. You need to keep praying, Son. And you need to listen … I mean really listen to what Jesus is trying to tell you."

CHAPTER 6 – Dreaming Big

As he hung by one arm, his left leg wrapped around a tilting ladder while the right dangled to the side, the only thing Don Beebe was listening to was his brother-in-law's words of reassurance.

"Whatever you do, my man, don't even wiggle," said Bob McQuade, standing on solid ground two stories below. "I've got to secure the bottom of the ladder first, so don't make a move."

Donny, holding on for dear life — or at least what was left of his pride — figured at that moment he was going nowhere but down.
And that was the problem.

It was four months after the Bears beat the New England Patriots in Super Bowl XX, and the only thing that had changed in Don's life was his mode of transportation to Bob's house.

Instead of chipping off ice from the windshield of his Cutlass, Don would jump on his blue 10-speed on these balmy late spring mornings, and bike the seven miles to his brother-in-law's house in Aurora's Fox Croft subdivision.

Normally he'd take the fastest route, pedaling along the Illinois 56/30 bypass, then get off the ramp at Galena Boulevard. His mom hated this route, convinced her son would get hit by a semi coming off the Interstate or by any one of the distracted commuters buzzing along the highway. After all, who would be looking out for someone on a bicycle at this hour of the morning?

To appease his mother, Don sometimes biked down Prairie instead. With sunrise so much earlier these days, he and Bob would get an early start on the day, showing up at the job site as early as 6 a.m. Now here it was, only 10:30 in the morning and he was already in trouble.

After his boss steadied the ladder so Don could make a slow descent to the ground, Bob suggested they take an early lunch. He was already plenty hungry, but he also figured his unhappy hang-man could use a little break before going back up the ladder.

Don wanted that break to be permanent. "Look, Bob, I really appreciate the fact you've let me work for you these past three years," he told his brother-in-law as the two men chomped on thick ham-and-mustard sandwiches. "But this isn't what I'm supposed to be doing. I know it sounds weird. And it's not like I'm conceited or anything. I've been thinking about this a long time … and I just know I'm supposed to be doing something with my life that involves sports."

Bob nodded. "I agree, Donny. You're a jock … a heckuva lot better jock than construction worker, that's for sure."

"Ya think?" Don retorted with a grin. "The problem is, I'm not sure what sport I should be playing."

"Let's face it, as good as you are on a basketball court, you would never make it in the NBA, not at five-foot-ten. But what about playing some pro baseball?" suggested Bob, who was convinced the world — perhaps even the universe itself — revolved around his beloved but hapless Chicago Cubs. "You might not be able to hit for power, but you've got a decent bat. And with that speed of yours, you could sure do some damage on the bases."

Don wasn't convinced. "I like baseball enough, I guess. But I've been thinking an awful lot about football again. Didn't know I'd miss it so much. And this whole season watching the Bears, I keep thinking, I could do that, you know? I could outrun those guys. I could catch those passes and run those routes."

The two men were sitting under the shade of a towering oak next to the 30-year-old home they were a half-day from completing. Wrens chirped somewhere in the branches and a robin danced at their feet. It was a lazy afternoon, but Don was restless and his thoughts were darting in a hundred different directions. "I need to get back in school," he said suddenly. "I need to start working out; put the cleats back on."

Bob chewed his way through the rest of the sandwich, then snapped his fingers as if he'd just hit upon an idea that would revolutionize the siding industry. His eyes flickered with animation but his face was dead serious. "The Bears are holding tryouts at their mini-camp next week. Why don't you give it a shot?"

Beebe stopped in mid-chew and stared at the other man. He swallowed hard. "What, are you nuts?" he asked. "I haven't even played a game of college football and you think I should try out for the Chicago Bears?"

"Why not?" Bob was smiling now — a wide, happy grin that encompassed his entire face. "I don't care how well they did this year, they can always use more speed."

It was stupid guy talk, for sure. But to two young siding men, whiling away some free time on a beautiful spring day, it somehow made sense. "When is that tryout? Don asked his boss. "And would you give me the day off?"

* * *

The following Tuesday, Don was surprised at how few people were in the stands as he walked toward the football field at Lake Forest College. The Bears camp was always well attended by the media, fans and casual spectators. But today, despite the pleasant temperatures and abundant sunshine, there was little action anywhere except on the field.

Beebe headed toward the thirty-yard line, where a throng of defensive ends, sweat already coating well-defined muscles, was running through conditioning drills. Don didn't see stop watches on anyone. It looked like a run-of-the-mill practice, as far as he could tell. He watched intently, his gaze skittering back and forth between the defensive linemen on the far side of the field as they grunted through their pass-rush drills, and the offensive line practicing mundane blocking techniques just a few feet from where he stood.

A thirty-something man, with a chiseled body that matched his square-jawed face, strutted toward Don. "Help you?" he asked curtly.

"Hey, how ya doing?" Don reached out his hand in greeting. "My name's Don Beebe and I just need to know when the tryouts begin. Do you know who I am supposed to check in with?"

The trainer — Beebe guessed his title by the words stitched across the left side of his shirt — ran his eyes up and down Don's diminutive frame. "Sorry, man, tryouts took place all day yesterday. Besides, they are invitation-only."

Don wasn't about to let this guy see his disappointment. "OK, thanks," he muttered, now feeling like a complete idiot. He retreated toward the parking lot. But 20 feet from his car, he turned back. Since he'd taken the time off from work, he might as well stick around and watch practice for a while. It was a spectacular day, and what else was he supposed to do except get in his car and drive back to his mundane life?

Don slid into a seat in the bleachers, shielding his eyes and wishing he'd brought a pair of sunglasses like the older man sitting a few rows up from him. Don shifted slightly to get a closer look at the spectator, one of the few in the stands. The man was unremarkable-looking — gray hair, medium build — yet something was familiar about him, even with his face mostly concealed by the dark shades and a wide-brimmed straw hat. VIP of some sort, Beebe figured, rotating another few degrees so as not to appear to be staring.

When the man removed his sunglasses to wipe away beads of sweat, Beebe recognized the face of Bill Tobin, general manager for the Bears. Don's mind started to churn. Should he? Did he dare?

Not exactly known for his chatty nature, Beebe's first impulse was to turn around and keep his mouth zipped. Don didn't like tooting his own horn. He had no idea how to sell himself to a college coach, much less the Bears head honcho. But Don wasn't thinking logically at this point.

"Mr. Tobin," he said, "Excuse me, but my name is Don Beebe and, well, sir, I used to play football back in 1983. For Western Illinois, actually. But I really didn't play for them because, well, sir, you probably don't care to know why ..."

Tobin's eyes narrowed but he said nothing.

"Sorry, sir, but I was just wondering if you could tell me how to go about getting a tryout with the Bears." There. He said it. He was already getting comfortable in his new role as idiot, so what the heck.

The man shoved his shades back into place, making it harder for Don to read his expression. No doubt it was one of amusement as he stared at the undersized young man sitting a few rows down with the gray sweats and faded black T-shirt advertising some siding company. Perhaps it was more like pity.

"We don't take guys off the street," Tobin said, a hint of kindness in his voice. "You have to be invited to camp, and those invitations usually go out to the very best college players. That's the way it works."

"What if I could run a 4.2 or 4.3 forty-yard dash for you?" Don asked. "Then would you sign me?"

Beebe couldn't believe the words popping out of his mouth. He'd never even been timed in the forty. He knew he was fast. And he figured he might fall somewhere in that range. Of course "might" can be a mighty big word.

Tobin removed his glasses again and this time his expression was a cross between annoyance and indifference. "Son, if you could run a 4.2 or 4.3, you'd already be in our camp — or someone else's."

"OK, thanks," Beebe said, then turned around. Tobin may have thought he was a goofball. But Don had all the information he needed. And that night he prayed extra hard.

"I know I can make it in the NFL, Lord. Just give me a sign ... something to tell me what I'm supposed to do next. Because seriously, Lord, all I'm doing right now is just hanging on."

CHAPTER 7 – Finding a Platform

His brother-in-law may have loved the cold, but Don was a much happy worker in the spring and summer, relishing the blazing sun that gave him an excuse to take off his shirt and allow rivers of sweat to freely run down his body.

Today, more than a month after his misguided "tryout" with the Bears, was another warm one as he and Bob worked on a new construction home on Baylor Street in Montgomery, a small village directly south of Aurora. Don was still plenty frustrated. He felt like a fool for thinking he could just show up at the Bears camp and expect to make an NFL team. Still, he couldn't forget what Tobin had said to him: "Son, if you can run a 4.3, you would already be on somebody's team." So, could he run a 4.3?

The question stuck in his head like an annoying Cindy Lauper song as he stood atop the staging while Bob worked the saw below. His brother-in-law had been on the ladder most of the day, so Don had volunteered to finish up the trim directly under the roof. After that last near fall, Bob had cut him some slack and kept him on the ground. But that only made Don feel guilty, and he forced himself back up on the staging, even volunteering, as he'd done today, to finish up some of the highest points on the houses.

Today, it proved to be a bad decision, especially as the wind continued to pick up all afternoon. Don, standing on the tip of his boots, was stretching to get the last few pieces nailed down on the third floor, when suddenly, a strong gust caught the staging. As the platform began to shift, Don, hunched under the roof, lost his footing and felt the panic begin to swell through his body. It grabbed his heart and rendered him all but motionless.

Seconds passed but it felt like eternity. Below, Bob, unaware of what was going on, continued cutting strips of aluminum as he belted out Madonna's "Like a Prayer" that the pop star also happened to be singing on the radio.

"Bob … Bob … Bob …BOB!" The wind muffled the call for help from above . Finally, Don's partner looked up and saw Beebe plastered helplessly to the side of the house, his feet inches above the wildly-swinging platform. "Hey man," he heard his employee whimper, "I can't move."

It didn't take Bob long to grasp this situation was different from some of Don's previous mishaps. "Donny, you're OK. Just drop down a little bit. The staging is right under you."

"Seriously, bro, you don't understand," came the response from above. "I can't move."

Bob lowered the saw and made his way to the ladder. He wanted to crack a joke, to distract Don with a little humor. But he quickly surmised this was no laughing matter to his buddy. "Then inch your way down the wall," he said evenly, "until you can feel your feet on the board."

Don didn't want to inch anywhere. The side of the house was now his security blanket. Let go of it and he was doomed. His fate, he was certain, would be a painful, slow, perhaps even bloody death.

"C'mon, Don, you can do this, man," Bob called up, his voice calm but insistent. "Just drop down, then grab the sides of the platform and crawl toward the ladder … I'll hold it for you."

With visions of mangled limbs dancing through his head, Don had no choice but to obey. Holding his breath, eyes tightly shut, he gradually lowered his body until he felt the still-rocking platform. Then, even more slowly, he dropped down on all fours, clutching the board tightly as he began the arduous crawl toward the ladder some 20 feet away.

Bob scampered up the rungs and balanced himself near the top of the ladder. He grabbed the platform to steady it. "I got it, Don," he called out. "You're fine. Just move slowly and don't make any sudden motions."

It wasn't until Don reached the ladder that his fear began to subside. But his heart still hammered in his chest, even after he reached the ground. He headed to the truck, opened the door and sat down on the passenger seat, wordless but clearly upset.

"You OK, bro?" Bob asked, offering a drink he'd pulled from the cooler. Don accepted the water but shook his head. "I can't do this anymore," he blurted. "I'll help you over the summer for sure, Bob. And I won't leave till you've got someone else to replace me. But I'm not going back up on that ladder again."

Just like that, Don canned his life as a tin man.

CHAPTER 8 – Getting Another Chance

Two weeks later, Don got the phone call from Western Illinois.

It was running-back Coach Mike Williams on the other end of the line. And he had a proposition. Crazy Coach Craddock had lightened up over the last few years. Yes, he was still nuts, but not certifiable.

"You've got two years of NCAA eligibility left," Williams told him. "And we'd really like to see you back because we know you could help this team in a big way."

"Seriously?" Don asked, still doubting the words of hope that seemed to have fallen out of the clear blue sky.

"Seriously," laughed Williams. "If you become a Leatherneck again, I promise personally to make sure Crad doesn't kill you; and that you'll be starting for us when the season begins."

That August of 1986, Don Beebe headed to Macomb again, this time more prepared to handle Crad's less-maniacal but still tough two-a-days. This time around, Don didn't puke once. He even gained a few pounds of muscle. Plus, his speed had indeed caught the attention of every Leatherneck coach. Not too many guys get a second chance like this, and Don was convinced it was God's hand directing this Western Illinois rerun.

But things aren't always as they seem. After busting his butt and celebrating the end of football camp a couple weeks later, a call came from NCAA representative Jim McKinney asking Don to see him ASAP — a request that is never a good sign, Don told himself on the short walk to the official's office. He was right.

"We just found out you are four-and-a-half hours short of being able to transfer to Western," McKinney told him from behind a desk piled high with the complex business of collegiate sports. "The only way you can play football here is by getting those credit hours from someplace else."

Don froze in his chair. "I'm sorry, I really am," said McKinney. "But it doesn't look like you're going to be able to play for us until you pick up a course or two from someplace else."

This time it was not Beebe's choice when he packed his bags and left Macomb. Surprisingly, Don didn't feel defeated. Nor was he all that upset. At least he had a clear direction. And he grew more determined than ever to stay the course.

Don drove home that same afternoon and the next morning enrolled at Waubonsee Community College in his hometown of Sugar Grove. He breezed through a semester at the local college on Route 47. Then he transferred back to WIU in the spring of 1987 to start classes, all part of the plan that would allow him to be on that football field the following August. So what if he'd lost another year? So what if he still had not played any college ball? He was focused and determined for the first time in years. And that felt mighty sweet.

Even his family was convinced this do-over would be a completely different experience. Although he still missed Diana, Don was older and considerably wiser. "Don't worry," he told his father the day he headed back to Western for yet a third time. "I know this chance to play college football is a gift. I'm not going to blow it again."

Don had no problems making it to classes, no matter how early in the morning they were held. And he didn't come up with excuses when it came to studying for tests. Except for working out with the team during spring drills, Don kept his nose to the grindstone, reminding himself each day that all this hard work and time away from Diana would pay off next semester.

"I know this is where I'm supposed to be," he told her. "The Lord's got a path for me that I need to follow. And I'm not taking any detours again."

Except for one.

After finishing up his last class on that overcast April day, Don deviated from his usual routine at the last second. Instead of walking around the Student Activities Center on his way back to the dorm as he did every day since he'd been back at Western, for whatever reason he cut through the building instead. That's how he happened to run into Nate Blanks, Albert Brown and Frank Winters. His three teammates, dressed in workout shorts and T-shirts, were headed to the field house to meet some NFL scouts who'd flown in to time standout seniors in the forty-yard dash.

NFL scouts. Right here at Western. Just a few hundred yards from where he was now standing in cut-offs and sandals.

Beebe could not believe his good fortune. He dropped his books not once but twice in his rush to get to Western Hall. Clutching the heavy texts, even as papers spilled from notebooks, he dashed into the building that housed WIU's basketball court and indoor track. He spotted receivers coach Brad Smith almost immediately and jogged over to where the assistant was scribbling on his well-worn clipboard.

"Coach, how come no one told me about this tryout? Did you forget I'm a senior?"

Smith glanced up, but only for a second. "Sorry, Beebs, these guys come here to watch certain players. They've got film on these seniors because they're all starters."

"But I can still run for them, can't I?"

Smith stopped scratching with his pencil and looked at the eager young athlete. "You may be a senior, Donny, but your problem is you've never even played a minute of college ball yet."

The coach could feel as much as see the young man's devastation. Smith glanced at Craddock, standing about twenty yards away and barking out orders to a linebacker who had showed up late.

"Check with Crad," he said. "See if Coach can use some of that undeniable charm of his to work you in."

The words were barely out of his mouth before Beebe was racing toward his head coach. "Coach Crad," he said, ignoring the older man's scowl at the interruption. "I'd like to run for the scouts, too. You know I'm fast. I'd really like to show them what I can do."

"Can't do it, kid," the head coach growled. "These guys are on a tight schedule, and besides, they already know who they want to look at."

"Coach, just ask 'em, would ya, please? All I need is a few seconds of their time. It's no big deal. Seriously, I can run. You know I can run."

Yes, Craddock knew the kid had wheels. And he and his staff had been working on plenty of plays that would exploit that speed when the season started the following August. But this wasn't the time or place to put Beebe's talents on display. And when Crad opened his mouth to respond, he had every intention of letting the kid down softly but firmly with a final no. Instead, he sighed. Craddock lumbered over to the half-dozen scouts bunched together near the track's finish line. Don could see the WIU coach's mouth moving, but he had no idea what the man was saying to the group.

All eyes turned to Beebe, standing half a field away. Don forgot to breathe. Finally, Craddock held up his hand and motioned to Don. "Get over here!" the coach boomed.

Beebe's grin was as wide as the goal post as he trotted over to the coach and visitors, only to have it disappear when he glanced down at the sandals on his feet. "Uh, one more thing, Coach. Can I run over to the dorm and get my shoes? I promise to be quick."

"Look, I'm in your corner on this one, OK? I got these guys to let you run. But they ain't gonna wait around for you one more minute. You want to show 'em what you got, you gotta do it right now."

Beebe knew when he had pushed to the limit. "Yes, sir," he replied. "And thanks, Coach. I owe you big time."

He waved his appreciation to the handful of scouts who had waited around to give him a shot. He spelled his last name for them, unaware no one bothered to write it down. The kid had on sandals, for crying out loud. Donny took his place on the starting line. Time seemed to stand still. He kicked off his footwear.

"Any time you're ready," said the St. Louis Rams scout, as he and five of his colleagues raised their stop watches.

Beebe bent over, feet slightly spread, right hand touching the ground. He stared straight ahead. He swallowed hard.

He exploded. Watches clicked. He flew, believing with all his heart that forty yards stood between him and his dreams.

It was all over in 4.32 seconds — a new record on Western's track. Beebe didn't know that at the time. He was just happy he didn't stub his bare toes.

A few minutes later, as he and his teammates gathered up their belongings to head back to the athletic center, Coach Smith jogged over to the players and motioned toward Don. One of the scouts wanted to talk to him. No one else. Just Don.

"Son, what's your name again?" asked the man with the Dallas Cowboys hat covering his graying hair.

"I'm Don Beebe, sir. B-E-E-B-E," he replied. This time the name went down on paper. "What's your number on the game film?" the scout asked.

"Sir, I don't have a number. I'm a fifth-year senior but I haven't been able to play football here yet."

The visitor's eyebrows shot up. "No kiddin'" he said. "So where did you play before? Junior college?"

Beebe shook his head. "I never played here or anywhere else before. I sat out and worked."

The scout shook his head and chuckled. "I've been doing this for twenty-one years and have never clocked someone this fast," he told Beebe. "We'll for sure be keeping an eye on you."

Don's head was spinning as he raced back to the dorm, and it wasn't until he opened the door to his room that he looked down at his feet and realized he'd left his sandals and books at Western Hall.

A few minutes later, he found his shoes, right where he'd taken them off. The books, however, were gone. But it didn't matter. This had been a great day, and nothing was going to wipe the smile from Don's face.

CHAPTER 9 - Facing New Rejection, Direction

Buoyed by this unexpected tryout and positive words from the scouts, Beebe went on to enjoy a kick-butt spring practice at Western, where he was moved from running back to wide receiver. Things were finally starting to look up for the Sugar Grove kid. But at the end of the camp, just as finals were wrapping up and students were heading home for the summer, the school's NCAA rep called Don into his office yet again.

By now Don was familiar with Jim McKinney's tone of voice when the news was not good. Even on the short walk from the dorm, Beebe still had plenty of time to create a list of somber possibilities. He walked into the windowless room and sat down. It was hot, stuffy, and the ceiling fan spinning overhead did little to help him breathe easier.

"I understand you've earned a starting job on the team this year," McKinney began. Don nodded as his heart slid into his throat. "Yes, sir, it's been a great camp."

"Problem is, you are a fifth-year senior and only now playing your first college football. And that has all the coaches a little nervous about how this is going to look to the NCAA. So we had to examine your situation closely."

Don's hands, folded in his lap, clenched into fists.

"I'm so sorry, Don, but it looks like you won't be eligible to play here," McKinney said. "I feel absolutely horrible about doing this to you again, but it's not just my decision."

Other platitudes followed, but Beebe did not hear them. The man behind the desk became a blur as tears filled Don's eyes. He wanted to yell. He wanted to hit something. He was being kicked out of school yet again. And this time he had no place to go.

Just that quickly, the journey had come to an end. Lowering his face into his hands, the young football player began to sob like a baby. McKinney looked on helplessly, hating his job at that moment, frustrated he could find no words of comfort.

The walk back to Wetzel Hall was possibly the longest trek of Don Beebe's life. Crossing the half-empty parking lot between the administrative offices and the eight-story dorm, he tried to keep the tears away. He failed miserably. The wind had picked up from earlier in the day, and teardrops flittered across his cheeks.

"Why, Lord?" he asked as he stared up at the sky. "Why did you help me get this far only to come up empty-handed?" None of this made any sense. Don felt as if he truly listened to what his Heavenly Father had been telling him. He had prayed hard and worked hard. He was convinced this was the direction he needed to take. Now he wasn't even sure what questions he was supposed to direct toward God.

Don's thoughts were broken by the shrill laughter of a young woman, her blond hair tied in a ponytail and both arms wrapped tightly around a lanky basketball player who had obviously said something amusing. The girl reminded him of Diana, and his heart hurt even more. The couple was only a few feet from him, but they might as well have been on another planet, their worlds at that moment were so vastly different.

Turning to avoid the couple, Don walked to the fence that separated the grass from the football stadium's turf. He stared out onto the empty field now roofed by a layer of clouds. He hadn't even gotten a chance to play one game here for the Leathernecks, he thought bitterly. All that work and not even one down in a real game.

"Lord, this can't be the end," he said. "There's got to be more to the story."

Time passed. Five minutes. Ten. It could have been longer. He felt the wind turn suddenly warmer. It rippled through his hair and dried his tears. Just as quickly, his heart felt lighter.

God, he truly believed, had the power to change the wind, to move the mountains. He knew that as surely as he knew he had to trust in his wisdom. "I don't know what your plan is, Lord," he confessed. "But I have faith you'll take care of it, and that you know what is best."

His heart still heavy, Don realized he had to get to Wetzel Hall. He had to start packing up his stuff. But how was he going to tell his parents? How was he going to break the news to Diana? Was he going to have to go back home and hang siding again? "Oh Lord," he prayed. "Please start telling me what I do from here. Because I really, REALLY don't want to go back up on that ladder again."

He called Diana as soon as he returned to his room. Try as he might, Don was unable to pepper any of his words with hope. He called his parents and was surprised the tears started flowing again. In between those conversations, he sat on the edge of his bed, staring blankly at the dorm walls that seemed to be closing in around him, suffocating the future he had so carefully constructed in his dreams. Only moments earlier he had felt God's presence, telling him to remain strong, to trust in the Lord. Now, here he was, growing more consumed by despair.

He prayed. He wept. He loaded up his car. He prayed some more. And just as he was about to turn out the lights in his room for the last time, the phone rang. Walking out the door, a bag of dirty laundry slung across his shoulder, he listened to its shrill jangle again. Why pick it up? It was probably family calling to tell him everything was going to be OK. But everything wasn't going to be OK. He was tired of talking about it. And besides, what could they say now that could possibly help?

He began to shut the door. But the phone continued to ring. And ring. And ring. *Answer it!* It was a voice inside him, asking to be obeyed. Don had heard the voice before. He knew it was the Holy Spirit speaking to him – telling him to pick up the phone NOW! He lifted the receiver.

"Don, am I glad I caught you," said McKinney, who had dismissed Beebe from school just five hours earlier. "Come over to my office, as soon as you can. I might have some good news for you."

He did, indeed. From the time Don had left his office to the time he got the phone call, the NCAA rep, troubled by the despondency he saw in the young man's face, had pored through the thick NCAA rules manual, skipping his lunch, hoping to discover a loophole or an overlooked ordinance that might save Beebe's football career.

"I think I finally found it," he said, pointing to small type on a page crowded with legalese. "Right here in black and white."

He read the passage. Don didn't comprehend the phrasing so McKinney put it into simple terms. "Turns out if a student-athlete leaves a school but returns to that same school, he is not considered a transfer student — regardless of how many other schools he attended. You are what's called a re-entry student. And that gives you another year of eligibility."

Don wondered if it would be appropriate to hug this man. Probably not. Instead, he pumped McKinney's hand so hard he was sure the poor guy would have to explain the black and blue marks to his wife that evening. "Thank you, sir. Thank you so much for taking the time to find a way for me to stay. You won't regret it. I promise you that."

On the way back to Wetzel, it hit Don. What had just happened was extraordinary; truly a God-thing. He stopped walking for a moment and bowed his head. "Thank you, Lord," he prayed, then made a vow he was going to work even harder to live up to this remarkable opportunity.

He made good on that promise.

Beebe went on to have an outstanding season with Crad's Leathernecks, earning Division I-AA All-Conference and All-American honors. And this time there was game film for these NFL scouts to review the following spring. The only problem was, with just a single season under his belt, the most any team would offer was picking him up as a free agent. That was fine with Beebe. All he wanted was a chance to work hard and prove himself again.

"There's another option that might be better for you," pointed out assistant coach Randy Ball. "You could try your shot at playing NAIA football — which stands for National Association of Intercollegiate Athletics. In this conference, athletes get ten semesters of eligibility, and it doesn't matter when or where or how they take them. That means you would have another two years of playing college ball."

That also meant two years to turn those die-hard dreams into reality. Beebe was pumped. He was packed. He was ready to continue his journey

First, he had to figure out where the heck an NAIA college was.

CHAPTER 10 – Ignoring the Obvious

Three weeks. Four bullet points. That pretty much summed up Don's plan of attack.

He was home for the 1987 Christmas holidays after finishing up the fall semester and his one and only football season at Western Illinois. Now he had until the first week of January to find the perfect NAIA school so he could get enrolled for the next semester and be eligible to play there that following fall.

His first requirement: The school had to be close to home. He liked his family way too much to only be able to see them one or two times a year. And besides, he was now engaged to the woman he had given that first romantic kiss to back in second grade.

Next, the school had to be on the national football radar so the scouts would come calling. Third, the team had to have had a good record the season before. Time was not on his side at this point, so Don didn't want to deal with a group of players struggling to gel. And fourth, for obvious reasons, the program had to feature a passing offense with a quarterback who could throw the ball.

Don and his dad did their homework. After researching all possible schools in a three-state area, they were certain they found the perfect fit at Illinois Benedictine University, just forty-five minutes east of Sugar Grove straight down I-88.

A visit to the school seemed to confirm that initial response. They both liked the coaches there and the facilities the program had to offer. And they were impressed with the passing offense the Eagles ran that earned them an 8-3 record the previous season. The returning quarterback had made All-Conference honors as a junior; and there was even another standout wide receiver on the roster that would keep the opponents from double-teaming Beebe.

"Seems to be a good fit," the elder Beebe said as he and Donny caught a bite to eat after touring the small but bucolic campus in Lisle, Illinois. Yet, even as he said the words, Don Sr. knew his son wasn't going to Benedictine.

"I like the coach. I like the school, Dad. But it's just not where I'm supposed to be." Don didn't know why he felt the way he did. He couldn't put his finger on the reason he didn't want to go to this highly-respected college that looked so good on paper. Whatever it was, his dad felt it, too. "I really think you need to pray on this," Beebe Sr. said.

A couple days later, Brad Smith called. The former wide receivers coach at Western was now heading up the football program at Chadron State. As soon as he heard Beebe was looking for an NAIA school, he decided to pull out all the recruiting stops.

"Chevron State ... Where the heck is that?" Beebe asked when Smith made that first contact by phone a few days before the trip to Benedictine.

"Not Chevron State," Smith said. "It's Chadron State. C-H-A-D-R-O-N but pronounced like SHADRON. Way up in the northwest corner of Nebraska. God's country out here, I'm telling you, Donny. Absolutely beautiful. I'll wait while you go grab an atlas so I can show you exactly where it is."

That turned out to be no small task. Putting the coach on hold, Beebe and his dad, more out of politeness than anything, opened up the book of maps and scoured the state of Nebraska. "I see Omaha. Here's Lincoln ... Grand Island. Dad, I can't find it? Can you?"

"Look up in the far corner," Smith said, after they took him off hold to help in their search. "Near the South Dakota border."

Both Beebe men laughed when they finally spotted Chadron, less than an hour from Mount Rushmore and far removed from any other dot on the state.

"The hunting and fishing are amazing," Smith continued pleading his case. "The sky is as blue, as clear as anything I've ever seen. And the people are so friendly. It's the kind of small-town feel you grew up in, Don. You would love it here, I know you would."

"I'll give it some thought," Don replied politely. "But honestly, Coach, it really doesn't fit any of the requirements my dad and I came up with. I appreciate your enthusiasm and the fact you want me to play ball for you. I'm just not sure."

Smith didn't give up. On his way home for the holidays in Sycamore, Illinois, he stopped by Sugar Grove. And this time he brought not just his unbridled passion, but also a couple dozen pictures, including photos of fish he'd caught at Isham Lake near the college. "I'm telling you, Donny: God's country. You would seriously love it here."

Something stirred in Don's heart. But he didn't like the feel of it — especially when Coach Smith went over all the important bullet points with the Beebe men – and not one of them fit their requirements. First and perhaps foremost, the college was not close. It was fifteen hours from home with no major airport anywhere nearby. Secondly, the team had won one lousy game last year. Inheriting only 21 lettermen, Smith was trying to rebuild the CSC football program from the ground up. Also, the quarterback was just a freshman, and a mere five feet, seven inches tall at that. Then there was the fact Chadron was hardly a nationally-recognized program. "So Coach," Don asked his enthused recruiter, "Have you ever had any players make it into the NFL?"

"Oh, absolutely," Smith replied eagerly. "Dub Miller. Back in 1935."

Donny locked eyes with his father. *You gotta be kidding,* the younger man's expression seemed to say. Don Sr. shot his son a quick glance as if to remind him that sometimes answers are not always so obvious.

As he lay in bed just hours after the coach left, Donny had but one request. "Please, God, don't send me to Chadron State. I like to fish, but the school doesn't fit even one of my requirements. Not one."

He continued his conversation with God, mostly begging for a sign that would point him away from Nebraska and back into his comfort zone. His prayers seemed to go unheard. Or more likely, he did more listening than talking.

In the morning Donny called Coach Smith. "Looks like I better get out my fishing pole," he said matter-of-factly. "I'm coming your way."

CHAPTER 11 – Going the Distance

It was closing in on ten at night and Don was tired, hungry and moving quickly toward a state of downright grumpiness. It had been hot and muggy on this July day, and the fifteen-hour car ride to Chadron State had taken a whole lot longer than the one he'd driven with his parents in January when he'd first enrolled for classes here.

That winter drive hadn't been much of a picnic either. The trip through the flat plains of Nebraska had turned into a seemingly endless journey of barren cornfields interspersed with barren wheat fields dotted by occasional blocks of barren pasture. And his enthusiasm had quickly waned. At one point, somewhere between Omaha and Lincoln, Don had begged his parents to turn the car around and take him back home. Of course his dad did no such thing. And Don started feeling better when they got to the Nebraska Panhandle, home of beautiful Chadron State Park. Still, when they came to a billboard that read "Welcome to Chadron, Population 5,200," they could see no signs of civilization — except for a South 40 Steakhouse offering all-you-can-eat buffet every Tuesday night.

"Let me know when we drop off the face of the Earth," Don had dead-panned from the back seat. "The ride to the bottom will probably be the thrill of the day." Five minutes later when the car had crested the hill, the town seemed to have popped out of nowhere, lying before them like a scene from a drugstore Christmas card. As they made their way through the small tidy downtown, the leafless trees lined the streets like good soldiers, inviting them into this strange but intriguing new kingdom.

Don felt his stomach knots loosen as the family drove down Main Street. The few people wandering about had waved and smiled at the new folks who had just arrived in town. Even other drivers would raise a welcoming hand in passing. "Friendly town," Don's mom had remarked. "And look at the park over there with the old-fashioned fountain."

In the weeks and months that had followed, Don found out Chadron was indeed a pleasant town. At least he could feel the genuine warmth from its residents the few times he'd venture off campus to eat in a local restaurant or drop in to pick up another pair of socks or a bottle of shampoo at the only department store.

Still, for most of that first semester there, Don had stuck close to campus. The first dorm he moved into, Edna Work Hall, was for older, married students and felt like a jail, cold as the concrete from which it was made. But after transferring to a more traditional room at Kent Hall, he quickly made friends, even with the students four years younger. Never a party animal, even in his earlier college days, he had arrived in Chadron with a singular goal, just as he'd done at Western a year earlier. Go to classes, crack the books and get eligible for the fall football season.

That meant sometimes life got mighty lonely. Even under the best of circumstances, he would have missed Diana like crazy. Not only were they engaged to be married, she was a whole lot further away than when he'd gone to Western. And spring drills are never any fun, even minus Coach Craddock.

Yet Beebe hadn't let the long nights and exhausting days deter him. He was laser focused now on that unlikely goal seeded during lunch with his brother-in law and sprouted while talking to the Bears general manager. Even when Diana would call and want to discuss their July wedding plans, Don would only listen to about 25 percent of her chatter. Others might describe his dream as a long shot; and in fact, a few had, even to his face. But Beebe didn't care. His vision was as clear as the fishing stream he'd found just a few short miles from campus: He knew he could play in the NFL.

That semester had passed quickly enough, and before he knew it, Don was back in Sugar Grove, picking out dinnerware patterns and trying on tuxes. On July 9th, he stood at the altar of Assembly of God Church in Aurora, and watched Diana walk down the aisle in a long dress of chiffon and taffeta that transformed her into an angel princess. He'd never seen her look so beautiful.

Now here he was — barely three weeks after saying "I do" — pulling into Chadron with his new bride and little brother Dan in the overstuffed Cutlass that was tugging an overstuffed U-Haul. His stomach was rumbling, eyelids dragging, back aching. But there didn't seem to be lights on in any of the restaurants or fast-food joints they had passed. And there was a "No Vacancy" sign out front of the one motel in town.

Not that they could have afforded to pay for a room. The newly pronounced Mr. and Mrs. Don Beebe had spent all their money on a week-long honeymoon in Hawaii, so they only had a hundred dollars between them. And until Diana was able to find a job, that cash had to stretch as far as possible.

Don drove aimlessly around the small, heavily-treed campus until he finally gave up and pulled into the parking lot of the football stadium. "Guys, I'm beat," he yawned. "Driving straight through like this is a killer, and I just want to find some place where I can close my eyes. I wouldn't even mind sleeping in the car tonight. Then in the morning we can go find Coach Smith and figure out what we're supposed to do."

He received no argument from his passengers, who had shared the driving on this cross-country trek. Right now, the back seat of the black Cutlass Supreme, even crammed with most of the trio's worldly possessions, looked inviting to Dan, who had been recruited to play basketball at Chadron.

"The parking lot is quiet and nobody's going to disturb us," his brother said, releasing his own wide yawn. "Let's just finish off the food and call it a night."

Barb's ham-and-cheese sandwiches, though they had ridden in a large cooler the entire trip, seemed as lifeless as the three Beebes. After they wolfed down the last of the nourishment, Dan scrunched into a ball in the back seat, Diana pulled a pillow next to her head on the passenger side of the front, and Don tried to make himself as comfortable as possible in the driver's seat across from her.

No one slept well. Around two in the morning Don, dressed in only a T-shirt and cut-offs, crawled out of the Cutlass and created a makeshift bed on the ground under a nearby tree. But as the temperature dipped into the fifties and with no blanket for cover, he retreated back into the car an hour later.

Don awakened to a tap-tap-tapping on the driver's window and a face peering in at him. Startled but with no room to even jump, he stared blankly at the woman, not yet awake enough to remember where he was and why a stranger was mouthing words that only gradually began to make sense.

"Are you kids lost or something?" the woman asked. She had kind eyes, like his mom's. "I was out on my morning walk and had to make sure you are all OK. Don't see too many people sleeping in cars around here, you know."

By now, with the sun beginning to rise over Chadron's football stadium, Don grasped where he was and why his whole body felt like he'd spent the night scrunched in a high school locker. "No, ma'am, we're not lost. We go to school here and we just got in late last night from Illinois so we thought we'd sleep here until I can meet with my coach and then..."

The woman's gray eyes crinkled, her lips parting into a grin. "You're Don Beebe, aren't you?" she interrupted. "I've been reading all about you, young man. And it's all good stuff. According to the paper, you're the one who is going to help our lousy football team win a few games." She glanced at the passenger. "Is that your new bride with you?"

Don, too, shifted his focus to Diana. Her eyes were glazed from lack of sleep, and her blond hair was tangled from a long ride and restless night. He reached over, touched her hand and grinned. "Yes, ma'am. I'm Don and this is Diana. And that's my brother Dan. He'll be playing basketball here."

The woman's eyes moved to the back seat, where Dan, still curled in a tight ball, his head resting on a black Hefty trash bag, had yet to show movement.

"We probably need to find Coach and tell him we're here," Don continued, "because we really don't have anywhere to go and he was going to help us find someplace, maybe even give us some ideas where Diana could get a job."

"You need a job? A place to stay?" The woman snapped her fingers together. "Well, I guess it's a good thing I was taking my morning walk and ran across you kids, because I think I might be able to help you with both."

Her name was Marlene Myers, and she and her husband Dick happened to be looking for someone to work in the drugstore they owned in downtown Chadron. "Let's go rustle up some breakfast for you guys," she said. "Then we'll help you find a place to live."

That part didn't take long either, since Marlene seemed to know everyone in town. By noon, Dan was unpacking his meager belongings in his eight-by-eight dorm room; and Don and Diana had settled on a one-bedroom 600-square-foot mother-in-law apartment located just behind a bigger house on Morehead Street. Their bed took up the entire bedroom; there was barely space for a table in the kitchen. And the bathroom was so small, Don could sit on the toilet and spit into the sink while brushing his teeth.

It worked out just fine, especially when he was in a hurry, as the young newlyweds usually were. Plus, it was only a hundred dollars a month, which was a strong selling point for the couple so low on funds.

But despite the many macaroni dinners and cold nights when they tried to save money by shutting off the heat, Diana came to love the friendly place as much as Don had. Chadron's small-town Midwestern values mirrored their own; and the folks here reminded them of the people they grew up with in Sugar Grove. Besides, even if they only had a few dollars to their name as they tried to keep one step ahead of the bills, they knew this was an important year; and that Chadron, Nebraska, was an important stepping stone to their future.

"I can't explain it," he told his young wife as they snuggled on the couch the night before his first football game as a Chadron State Eagle. "Here we are, in this little town in the tip of Nebraska and I'm not really sure how we got here. I just know it feels right."

"I believe you ... and in you," Diana said, snuggling closer to her new husband. You're going to have a great game tomorrow."

* * *

The next day, under a radiant prairie sky, Don Beebe watched his young quarterback throw five interceptions in the first half of the game against South Dakota Tech.

"You're letting the pressure get to you," he told Steward Perez at halftime. "Forget about the home crowd. Forget the trash talk. Just concentrate on your timing. You do it every day at practice. Get the ball to me and I'll take it into the end zone."

Perez knew his wide receiver could outrun anyone on the field. The quarterback looked into Beebe's face as the two athletes stood face to face. Perez could have sworn Don's eyes grew two shades darker.

"Stay open," he told Beebe. "It's coming your way."

Don made good on his promise. No. 5 scored two easy touchdowns that game, and it became apparent to almost every football fan in the stadium this All-Conference player from Illinois could go deep any time he wanted. The final score: Chadron State 35, South Dakota Tech 21. Beebe had five catches for almost sixty yards, ran for another twenty and returned two kicks for ninety yards.

It was good enough for a win, but not enough to earn the respect of the coach of the following week's opponent. "Listen to this," Don told Diana as he held the paper that featured an interview with Black Hills State Coach Larry Sommers. 'We're going to shut Beebe down. We've got players as fast as he is, and we don't have any plans to do anything differently this week against him."

Diana shrugged. "I guess the word hasn't gotten to him how ridiculously competitive you are. I'm also guessing he's not actually seen you run. We'll see what he has to say after Saturday's game."

Very little, as it turned out. The following week, Beebe caught four touchdown passes and ran an eighty-nine-yard- kickoff return into the end zone. And game after game it became obvious Don Beebe played at a whole different level than his NAIA peers. Yet the majority of Beebe's most spectacular plays went unrecorded in the photo files of Chadron State history. Information Director Con Marshall would try time and time again to get shots of the school's star player for publicity purposes. But by the time he'd focused his lens from quarterback to the wide receiver, No. 5 was already down the field and in the end zone.

"Hey, it's not like I haven't been trying," he told the head coach when Smith complained about the lack of film. "But it was like trying to catch a jet plane streaking across the sky."

Nothing, it seemed, could slow Beebe down.

CHAPTER 12 – Hitting it Hard

The sixth game into the season featured the longest bus ride of Beebe's collegiate career — and the most painful. He and his team bounced along in the smelly old Greyhound for fifteen hours — through Little Bighorn, where General George Armstrong Custer made his famous Last Stand — to Helena, Montana, home of the Carroll College Fighting Saints.

The game against this NAIA powerhouse was a defensive power struggle, as well. The Saints had, as Chadron's opponents usually did, double-teamed Beebe. And Perez, although he had developed more confidence from earlier in the season, still struggled to find his rhythm, especially when his offensive line wasn't coming off the snap as quickly as needed.

But Beebe was beginning to understand the upside of patience. Right before halftime, it paid off when Perez, on a third and eight, fell back with time to spare, looked to his left, then fired the ball toward Beebe, who, twenty-five yards away, was flying across the middle. At the same moment Beebe cradled the football, a towering linebacker rammed him, T-boning the receiver with a POP! that could be heard in the top row of the bleachers.

The hit to the gut upended Beebe. He flipped over the six-foot-two defensive player and landed on the back of his head. He folded like a sandwich, with hips and legs shoving directly into his shoulder pads.

Beebe heard the crack before he felt the pain. Neither the sound nor the feeling was familiar to him. He rose slowly from the ground and finished two more plays before walking off the field as the first half of the game ticked down. His hip stung like an attack from a swarm of hornets, but mostly he felt a raw soreness in his throat. Still, he kept quiet as the team ran into the locker room at halftime. When the head coach and offensive coordinator asked how he was feeling, he declared he was "good, feeling good."

Beebe made it through the third quarter, accumulating more than one hundred receiving yards . But as he sprinted back to the huddle after making his seventh catch of the game, Don looked down and noticed a peculiar sight. His throat was jutting out as far as his chest.

He raised his hand to the swollen skin. It felt like Rice Krispies.
He finished the play and made a bee-line to Brad Smith. "Coach," he gurgled, "I think I did something to my throat."

Smith, staring at his star player, felt his stomach lurch. He remained expressionless, determined not to panic in front of the kid as he motioned for the trainer. Two minutes later an announcement boomed from the stadium loudspeaker: "If there is a doctor in the house, please report to the Chadron State sidelines immediately."

Don gingerly massaged his swollen throat, wondering if he should feel more pain. He really wanted to be out there on the field running routes for Perez instead of waiting for medical help. It didn't take long for a middle-aged man, dressed in khaki pants and a tan trench coat, to trot over from the home team bleachers. He announced himself as a doctor, ran his fingers over Don's throat for a couple seconds, then quietly ordered the trainer to get the ambulance as close to the bench as possible.

"Looks like you ruptured your larynx," he finally said. "No need for alarm, but you've got air bubbles filling your throat. And that means we need to get you to General immediately."

With four minutes and twenty-eight seconds left in the game, Beebe was whisked to the emergency room. There, the doctor ordered an anti-inflammatory medicine for the ruptured muscles. Two hours later, sporting a brace around his neck, Beebe checked out of the hospital and returned to the bus, where his team, hungry but concerned, waited for news of Beebe's condition and the delayed post-game meal.

Don thought the fifteen-hour bus ride to the game was long, but it was a trip to the neighborhood park compared to the excruciating trek home. And it didn't help that, sitting next to the coach in the front of the bus, he couldn't take part in the pizza orgy going on behind him. The pain, he noted sourly, had even dulled his appreciation for pepperoni and sausage.

Two hours into the ride was when the real fun began. As the bus bounced along Interstate 90 under the dark, starless night, a cramp hijacked his right hamstring with no warning, ripping through his muscle with the fierceness of a gladiator's sword. Don screamed out, startling his almost-sleeping coaches. "Beebs, for crying out loud, what's the matter?" Smith asked. "CRAMP," he grimaced, the pain continuing to escalate.

Smith jerked to attention and scooted next to his wide receiver. "You're going to have to get up, Donny," the head coach ordered, "You need to work the cramp out or it's not going to get any better."

But Beebe couldn't get up; in fact, he couldn't move at all with the brace constricting most of his upper body. The tightness migrated to his left hamstring and Don wanted to cry out again.

Smith winced as he looked into the young man's contorted face. "We need to get Don on the ground. Jerome! Corey! Help me get him on his back. Make some room so we can lay him in the aisle."

Don was in too much agony to know or care that he was being forced onto his back. As one pair of large hands hiked his coat and shirt over his head, another pair pulled down his pants and placed bags of ice on his constricting hamstrings.

By now, every player, coach and trainer on the bus was wide awake, as teammates collected coats for a makeshift pillow and blankets for their injured teammate. Beebe felt like his entire body was slowly making its way through a dull meat grinder. He wasn't about to give in to the pain. And he sure as heck wasn't going to think about this situation being anything more than a temporary inconvenience. Although the cramping leg and ruptured larynx rendered him next to speechless, Beebe struggled to get one message across loud and clear.

"Just so you know, Coach, I'm playing next week."

Smith wanted to roll his eyes, but refrained. "We'll see, Beebs. Right now we just have to get you home to Diana in one piece. And the way it stands now, she's not going to be all that happy when she sees the shape we returned you in."

The bus rolled into Chadron at two in the morning. When Diana saw him being helped down the steps, her eyes moistened. She'd been listening to the game on the radio and knew Don had been transported to the hospital. From that point on, she'd been in contact with Smith and the emergency room doctor. Still, she wasn't prepared for how pathetic her young husband looked as he was helped off the bus by a trio of his teammates.

"Honey, I don't know if I can do this," she admitted on the chilly ride home. "I spent the entire day wondering if you were in one piece, wondering if they were telling me the truth about your injury. And then when get home, you look even worse than I imagined."

"Get used to it, Di," he said. "And just so you know, I'm playing next week."

Diana took her eyes off the road long enough to shoot a glare his way. "You have to be kidding me!" Her tone was more of disbelief than anger. He got the same reaction from Dr. Cliff Hanson when he checked in with the team physician the next morning. "I've got to be out on the field next week," he told the doctor. "I can't be missing any games at this point in the season."

"Then if you play, you've got to wear a brace," Hanson ordered. That wasn't what Beebe wanted to hear. "Doc, that's not going to work. Not only do I need to be out there for kickoff, I have to perform at my very best. And there's no way I can do that with a brace around my neck."

The doctor didn't agree with the young athlete's resolve, but he respected it. One way or another, this kid was going to play. "If your coach says it's OK," he said, shaking his head slowly, "I'll sign the release."

That next game was a hard-fought battle with Montana Tech. Beebe had seven catches for 157 yards and two touchdowns. It didn't seem to matter he was still nursing a shattered larynx the following game. He had other issues that were causing even more problems. During practice that week, he'd also wrenched both ankles. But he didn't bother telling his coaches, fearing he'd be put on the DL list. He simply wrapped both legs and ended up adding another 138 yards and two more touchdowns to his already impressive stats.

Beebe finished that 1988 season for Chadron State with 906 catching yards, and returned kicks for another 676 yards. They were good enough numbers for the Omaha World-Herald to name him Nebraska Football Player of the Year. Those stats were also good enough to catch the attention of a few NFL scouts.

Smith wasn't surprised when he and his star player started hearing from a few teams. Some letters showed up in the mail; Don even talked to a couple of scouts on the phone. But only one man from the NFL went to see the speedster on the prairie for himself. Bill Giles, who scouted for the NFL Combine, which represented all twenty-eight teams, lived in Nebraska. Still, it was no easy task getting to Chadron, as he noted on that lonely stretch of highway that led into town.

As exhausted as he was when he finally arrived, Giles' eyes opened wide when he read the numbers on the stop watch after timing Don in the forty-yard dash. 4.28 seconds. "I can't write that down as your time," he told Beebe after the young man asked how he'd done. "If you don't run as fast for the other scouts, it'll be my reputation on the line."

Instead, he wrote 4.38 seconds. "I hope this is enough to get you a Combine tryout," he said, his tone still one of disbelief. "I'm going to try to make that happen. But it'll be tough. You're fast but you're unknown. Unfair or not, it's going to be an uphill battle."

CHAPTER 13 – Receiving the Invitation

It's not like the letter was totally unexpected. Still, when Diana pulled it out of the mailbox, along with a stack of utility bills and a wish-you-were-here card from her sister, her hands began shaking so hard she dropped all the letters into the filthy pile of snow at the end of the driveway.

Diana wasn't aware of the cold as she stooped down to pick up the scattered mail. A blanket of sleet could have hit her in the face at that moment and she wouldn't have felt a thing – except the thrumming of her heart.

She stared at the letter, unaware her nose and fingers were turning red. Don was on campus — probably sitting in Professor Benson's statistics class right now — and there was no way to get in touch with him until he popped home for lunch, as he did every Monday, Wednesday and Friday. Could she wait that long? "Please, please, please," she whispered as she clutched the white envelope with the NFL logo in the left corner. "Please let this be the news we want."

Whatever words the letter contained, Diana wanted Donny to read them first. She ran inside, threw the envelope on the tiny kitchen table, next to the strawberry-shaped napkin holder they'd received as a shower gift from her sister Brenda, and tried not to think about what the next hour or so would mean. Like that was going to work.

She pulled a pile of white socks out of the laundry basket and concentrated on matching them — a daunting task even when her mind was not so preoccupied. Two ankle socks, one with ribbing around the top, one without. Three mid-calf, one with red trim, one with a Nike swoosh, one with a black symbol of some sort that was no longer readable. None that matched. Four knee-lengths. Two orphans. Two mates. Progress, she noted wryly.

Diana kept her eye on the clock. Ten minutes until Donny came home. She pushed aside the socks and began to sort T-shirts: short sleeves on one pile; sleeveless on another.

At exactly 11:28, she heard her husband's car pulling into the driveway. She jumped off the couch, knocking her orderly piles onto the freshly vacuumed floor. Diana couldn't wait for Don to walk through the door. Every day for the past two weeks he'd arrived home from classes and asked the same thing: "Anything in the mail?" Today she would get to tell him what he wanted so badly to hear. Diana grabbed the envelope off the table and flew out the front door, her arms flailing as she neared the still-running car.

"What the heck are you doing without your coat?" Don asked as he opened the driver's door.

"It's here, Don!" Diana gushed, thrusting the letter at him. "It's from the Combine!"

The NFL Combine, a group of scouts representing all teams, only invites the best college seniors in the country for a special tryout. There in Indianapolis, these top prospects would be tested in agility, strength and speed. It was a place where the best of the best could strut their stuff in front of pro football's VIPs. It was a unique stage to prove that all the hype these athletes had enjoyed all season was not an illusion; that they had what it takes to play on Sunday afternoons in front of thousands of rabid fans, not to mention millions of TV viewers.

His eyes darted from the envelope to her face and then back to the letter. "Did you open it?" he asked, his voice remarkably steady.

"No, I wanted you to do it." Diana replied, her soft answer a stark contrast to the heavy hammering inside her chest.

Don forgot about the fact his wife was shivering. "Please, Jesus," he prayed as he held the paper in his hands. "Give me the strength to be able to deal with whatever this letter contains. And if it is your will, let it be the words I want it to be."

Diana uttered a quick "Amen." Don only stared at the envelope. "Open it! Open it, Donny, for crying out loud, it's cold out here," Diana begged, her arms now wrapped around her body.

Don tore open the envelope. He pulled out the paper inside, unfolded it and scanned the first line.

His hands trembled as he read aloud: "Dear Don Beebe. You have been invited to attend The NFL Combine on February 23, 1989, at the RCA Dome in Indianapolis, Indiana ..." He got no further before his wife grabbed him around the neck and let out an unladylike whoop. Don, still clutching the letter, threw his arms around Diana. Neither of them knew whether to laugh or cry, so they did a whole lot of both as they clung to each other with the letter now crushed between them.

"This is it, honey," Don finally said. "This is what we've been praying for. It's going to give me a chance to go up against the best and to see if I really do have what it takes to reach my dream."

The couple went into the house; and Don, not bothering to shed his coat, called home to let his parents know the good news. His eyes misted again as he heard the pride in his dad's congratulations. And he laughed out loud as he listened to the delighted screams of his mother in the background. Then, as Don read the letter again to his brother a few minutes later — he would read it to himself a hundred times before going to bed that night — he felt the pressure slowly begin to mount. Yes, this was the chance he had always dreamed of. But now it was up to him to do something with it. So, what if he couldn't? What if he couldn't run the routes? Or catch the passes? What if he ran as fast as he could and they told him he just didn't have what it takes?

Diana knew what he was thinking. "Don, you are going to Indianapolis and turn all those NFL scouts and coaches into believers. You are talented. You are fast. You belong with the best because you are the best."

"You don't understand, Di," he replied. "All the work up until now only gets me to the party. The bar has been raised and I have to be ready to go that high or I'll be sent packing as soon as I get there."

The next few weeks were a blur as Don tried to concentrate on his classes and continue to work out in the crowded gym of the Nelson Physical Activity Center. He could think of little else except the Combine tryout. What would he need to bring with him? Who would be there? What tests would he have to perform?

As intense as his training was before, now it was doubled. Instead of working out once a day for a couple of hours as he did during the season, he would rise before dawn when the rest of the campus was still asleep, and run through the frigid streets of the small town. Then he would go to classes, dart home, grab a sandwich, and hit it again in the afternoon, working on the lunges he designed himself to increase the power in his hip flexor muscles.

But that was just the conditioning stuff. For a couple more hours each day, he'd catch passes from Perez and run routes against Jerome Hyatt, a talented defensive back by NAIA standards but too small for a legitimate shot at an NFL career.

"If it's not me, I'm glad it's you," Jerome said one evening as the two athletes sat on parallel benches in the outdated weight room after an arduous set of drills. "Getting to the Combine is the stuff we all dream of, you know. We're proud of you, Beebs, because no one deserves this more than you."

Don thanked his teammate. He leaned forward and stared down, focusing on the beads of sweat that dropped from his forehead onto the grubby floor. Beebe's thoughts were hundreds of miles away so he didn't hear his friend's whispered response.

"But, man, Beebs," Jerome shook his head and laughed, "Would I love to be in your shoes."

CHAPTER 14 – Hitting the Wall

Don didn't take this amazing opportunity for granted, not for one second. Which is why his focus only intensified as the Indianapolis date grew closer. Diana, working at the drug store sometimes six days a week to keep ahead of the bills, knew when he became this preoccupied to give him space. She didn't say a word when she would come home from the store to find him sitting on the couch in the dark — TV off, books closed. And she tried not to take it personally when she'd chatter away about her day at work and then, five minutes later, realize he hadn't heard a word she'd said.

For seven years she and Donny had been best friends, which meant she probably understood him better than he understood himself. She was acutely aware of his competitiveness, his intensity. Still, just because she understood it didn't mean she'd not grown weary of seeing him so moody, so preoccupied. She was working long days, often evenings, too. Diana was tired of the bitter cold, the unrelenting snow. And she missed her home, her family and her friends. She was a social creature, and living here in Chadron these past six months had been hard at times. Really, really hard.

The night before Don left for Indianapolis, Diana had just started making dinner — scrambled eggs and toast because money was getting tight again — when she decided to throw out an idea she'd been toying with all day. "Don, you need to relax a little bit, just for tonight. We haven't gone out, only the two of us, for a long time. Why don't we splurge and go out to eat, then catch a movie? Or maybe we could just go for a nice moonlight walk in the snow."

She flashed him one of her wide grins and grabbed his hand. "C'mon, Donny. We won't be out long. And it would be kind of romantic to go on a real date again."

Her husband shook his head. "I've got a lot to do before I leave tomorrow, and I don't think I can concentrate on anything else right now."

Don's words irritated her. She'd already washed up all the clothes he was taking to Indianapolis. She'd even packed them in the scuffed, smelly gym bag he was taking. "What do you have to do for tomorrow, besides brush your teeth and go to bed?" she asked, her smile wavering.

"Diana, you don't understand," he replied, his eyes darkening. "It's not the physical stuff I have to do. It's the mental stuff. I need to relax; take it easy so I can focus on tomorrow. I don't need to go see a silly movie or take a walk in the park to relieve stress."

Diana knew her husband's words weren't meant to be unkind. But they stung anyway.

"I didn't know spending some quality time with me was silly," she said, tears filling her eyes. "Believe me, Donny, I'm not trying to ruin your focus for this tryout. I'm just trying to help by giving you a chance to have a little fun. Besides, it would be nice for me to get out once in a while." Diana's voice had become noticeably shaky. "I know I'm not the one who is going to get timed in the forty tomorrow. But that doesn't mean this is not affecting me, as well. And sometimes I think you are losing sight of the fact we're in this together. Together, Don. In everything."

Don understood his young wife well enough at this point to know when she had reached her limit. And he also knew the best thing he could do was take her in his arms, tell her everything was going to be OK; that he loved and appreciated her very much. Then both of them would leaf through the paper to find a good flick.

But as was too often the case, at least if you asked his mom, Don's stubbornness won out over common sense. "I love you, Diana, but I can't believe you don't get how important this is to me. This is my future. Our future. And right now I need to think about only one thing."

"As usual, that doesn't include me," she retorted, her voice now sharp as even more tears threatened to complicate the already tense showdown.

"C'mon, babe, I can't deal with you crying right now. In fact, that's the last thing I need."

"Don, don't you hear yourself?" Diana threw down the waste basket she'd just emptied. It sounded like a shot from a .22 as it hit the floor. "When it comes to football, it's always about your needs. Ever since I've known you, I've had to deal with your world and how it revolves around sports. Do you ever stop and think about how selfish that can be? Have you thought about what I've had to give up so you can follow your dreams?"

By this point, both voices were raised beyond the conversational tone. Don's stare could have cut through stone. Diana returned the icy gaze. Finally, Don spoke.

"You know what? I just won't go to the tryout tomorrow. It's obviously taking a toll on both of us, and I can't go to Indianapolis knowing how miserable you are."

Diana wasn't in the mood to go on any guilt trip. "Don't put this on me, Don. I'm not asking you to not go. You know good and well how excited I am about this opportunity. I'm just asking you for a little more time for us. Us, Donny. You and me together."

As Diana turned and stormed into the bedroom, slamming the door behind her, Don called after her, "Fine, run away and pout," he groused. That just shows how immature you really are."

He whirled in the opposite direction and stomped toward the front door. Before throwing it open, Don drove his right hand into the wall with a fierceness that surprised him more than the bolt of pain that shot up his arm.

He didn't care. Don slammed the door even louder than his wife had closed the one to their bedroom. And it wasn't until a cold blast of air hit him full force that he realized he was only wearing a thin T-shirt in a fifteen-below-zero wind chill.

He walked in the direction of his brother's dorm. It was a good mile hike, but he didn't know what else to do. He was mad. Mad at Diana for not understanding where his head was. Mad at himself for being so insensitive to her needs. Mad that he'd let the argument get out of hand. Mad that he didn't know how to walk through that bedroom door and make everything all right again. He loved her so much, and nothing was as important as the two of them together. Not even this NFL tryout.

He was a jerk. A stupid jerk. Who happened to be very, very cold.

By the time Don knocked on his brother's dorm door, the icy air had turned his face as red as his swollen hand. "What the heck?" Dan muttered when he saw his unexpected visitor.

"I'm not going to Indianapolis tomorrow," Don mumbled, as he paced the room like a caged leopard. "I just had a huge fight with Diana, and I can't go with her mad at me. I need to stay here to patch things up."

Dan couldn't believe what he was hearing. His brother and Diana never fought. And to do so on the eve of this important tryout with the NFL was nothing short of ludicrous. But he wasn't about to let Don throw away everything he'd worked for, no matter what was going on in the little apartment on Morehead.

"Don, you may be older than me, but I've got to tell you, you're acting like a big baby," Dan said. "So calm down, then sit down and I'll get you something warm to drink." He practically shoved his brother onto the couch. "Hot chocolate, coming up. And throw on a blanket, for crying out loud. You're making me cold just looking at you."

A few minutes later, while handing his unexpected visitor the hot mug, he noticed Don's hand. "For crying out loud, what the heck did you do? Take a swing at Diana?" Dan grinned, because the very thought of his brother hitting his wife was laughable. Still, he was glad when Don smiled back.

"No, but I did something about as crazy: hit the wall on my way out. Didn't put a hole in it, though — at least I don't think I did. Guess that's something to be proud of."

Dan wasn't sure if he should delve into the reason for the fight. "Look, Donny, you need to go home and smooth things over with Diana. You know good and well that whatever it was you guys fought about is no big deal. Couples go at it sometimes. And the last thing either one of you wants is to miss this chance to play professional football."

Don, massaging his damaged hand, started to protest. "The pressure …. Everything all coming at once … You don't understand what a jerk I was."

His brother broke him off. "Finish your cocoa, then we'll drive your miserable butt back to your house. Or better yet, call Diana right now and tell her you love her, that you are sorry and that you need a ride. Whatever you do, you're going to Indianapolis tomorrow — even if I have to strap you to the top of the car and drive you myself."

CHAPTER 15 – Competing Without Sole

As Don slid through the fancy revolving doors of the Crowne Plaza Hotel in Indianapolis, he took in the large white pillars, marble floors, granite tables and crystal chandeliers. He knew he should probably be dazzled. Or maybe frazzled. Or at the very least, a little anxious as he looked over the star power that seemed to be taking up every square inch of space in that plush gold and red lobby.

"Whoa!" he said aloud. "Not exactly the Cowboy Inn in Chadron, Nebraska."

Fortunately, Beebe was too naïve to be nervous and too tired to be all that impressed. He'd gotten up at three that morning for the two-hour car ride to Rapid City, South Dakota, thankful his hand was not seriously damaged. From there he caught a plane that took him to Lincoln, then on to Chicago, where he had a couple-hour layover before climbing aboard a jet to Indianapolis.

With little more than cab fare in his pocket — and no idea he was even supposed to tip the driver after he got dropped off at the hotel — Don strolled alone through the expansive lobby. It was filled from one end to the other with reporters and cameramen focused on muscle-bound jocks wearing intense stares and high-dollar Nikes, flanked by leggy women and fast-talking agents.

Those women — he'd never seen so many fur coats in one room — didn't have a lot to say. But the agents were busy as flies in a cow pasture, chattering and swarming about as they made sure their clients had the right kind of equipment ... and that they were getting enough face time with the names that mattered most.

Don immediately recognized some of the big-time college players. Barry Sanders from Oklahoma State: Troy Aikman from UCLA: Tony Mandarich from Michigan State: Derrick Thomas from Alabama. And of course, there was Deion Sanders from Florida State, who rolled up in a limo, and stepped out wearing black leather, ropes of gold and an air of confidence that declared him the undisputable toast of the town.

Those highly sought-after prospects were the sure bets in this year's impressive NFL draft roster. Or at least as sure as anything can be when you're dealing with high-octane egos, full tanks of testosterone and the distinct possibility that at any given moment the dreams and dollars can all come to a screeching halt with just one hard hit.

But Chadron State star Don Beebe didn't have any agents holding his hand or hovering around him at this crucial junction in his life. And he certainly didn't have any of the fancy gear most of these prospects were modeling as they strutted about the hotel.

His Combine roommate, Mike Barber, a wide receiver from Marshall University, was one of them — all decked out in new Nike gear, shiny black jogging pants and matching jacket, both of which featured orange and gray stripes snaking down the sides. "So where you from, Don?" he asked, after the two shook hands.

"Chadron State. Ever heard of it?" Don asked, knowing full well what the answer would be.

"Chadmon what? No offense, man, but where the heck is that? Division II?

By now Don was used to this sort of response. "Chadron, C-H-A-D-R-O-N. It's up at the northwest tip of Nebraska. Tiny school. It's an NAIA school, if you know what that even means."

"NAIA," Barber repeated. As in Not All Important Association?"

He grinned. "Just kidding. Hey, you're here, man, and that's all that counts."

A knock at the door interrupted the conversation. Special delivery from Barber's agent; four boxes, each with a familiar swoosh on the package. "All right!" Barber grinned as he ripped open the first package and pulled out a pair of spanking new orange and white Nikes.

"Fit like leather gloves," he declared, after lacing up the first pair of turf shoes. "And it looks like I have enough to wear a different pair with every drill. Pretty crazy, huh? Your agent line you up with any cool stuff?"

"Are you kidding? I don't even have an agent," Don said. "To be honest, I'm not quite sure how to go about getting one."

"Oh, you don't find them; they find you. At least if you're good enough." Almost immediately, Barber realized how rude his comments sounded. "Sorry again, man. I seem to be putting my foot in my mouth a lot with you. Seriously, I don't mean that just because you don't have an agent you're not, like, good. Heck, you're probably more than good if you got here from that NINA school — or whatever it was — without any help."

Barber glanced at the shoes Don was now pulling out of his duffle bag. "Please tell me you're not wearing those," Barber said, eyeing the loose tread at the bottom of the right sneaker.

"The only ones I got," Don replied, tossing the scuffed and dingy gray ASICS onto the bed. The shoes, a twenty-nine-dollar pair he'd bought in high school, were so dirty and worn, he now used them for just about everything, including fishing and carrying out the garbage.

"You know, if you want, you're welcome to borrow some of mine," Barber offered. "I can only put on one pair at a time, after all."

Don shook his head. "Hey, man, that's nice of you. But I think your foot's a little bigger. Besides, I'm used to these babies. They're worn in pretty well, as you can see."

Barber picked up the right shoe and flicked the tread that was hanging half-on, half-off. He frowned. "This ain't good, dude. No matter how much you love these sorry things, they're not going to help your cause."

"I could try to glue the flap back on," Don suggested.

Mike shrugged. "Glue it or just yank it all off."

The decision was made for Beebe when he couldn't find any adhesive in the hotel. If he pulled the tread off, who knows? The whole bottom of his shoe might go with it. But Don wasn't all that worried. He knew he could run, and he knew he could run without having on a pair of fancy shoes. Or even ones with soles securely attached. But could he run fast enough?

That night, while some of the players were being wined and dined in the company of the Barbie Doll women, Don stayed in his room and called Diana. "I'm holding up fine. Just hope my shoes do, too," he told her. "I love you, babe. And I already miss you like crazy. But I feel good about this. I really do."

Don fell into an exhausted sleep that night, and awoke to what he knew would be the most important day in his life. After a continental breakfast, the athletes were bused over to Hoosier Dome, where they were put through a battery of medical tests from all twenty-eight team doctors.

"Jump on the scale, young man ... Stick out your tongue and say ahhh ... Pee in the cup...Roll up your sleeves and tighten your fist." It reminded Beebe of a herd of cattle getting ready for auction as they were poked and prodded and checked for everything from high blood pressure to hangnails, or so it seemed.

The real fun began the following day, as the prospects were divided into groups, depending upon their prospective positions, to determine overall athletic prowess. Beebe may have been a no-name from an even lesser-known college, but he quickly made an impression when he went up 38½ inches in the vertical jump, the third highest recorded at that year's Combine. And he opened even more eyes when he set a new record by breaking eight seconds on the four-corner drill, which, before the NFL did away with it, tested speed and agility running forward, sideways and backward.

Not that he knew any of this at the time. With little fanfare and few words, the hundreds of coaches, scouts and other officials simply took measurements, recorded times and jotted down notes as the athletes went from cone drills to shuttle runs to bench presses and long jumps.

Beebe was confident he was at least holding his own in the tests that mattered most for him. Later in the week, when the wide receivers were called to run passing routes, his confidence didn't wane, even going up against the likes of the two Sanders phenoms.

"Don't drop the ball. Don't drop the ball," he muttered over and over as he took off downfield after the pigskin was released. And he didn't. Each one that was lofted into the air, whether the throws were long spirals or short snaps across the middle, connected with his outstretched arms and he snagged them with little or no effort.

Then came the most-hyped test – the one that garners the most attention from officials, fans and the media alike – the forty-yard dash. For only the third time in his life, he was getting timed on this all important skill. But he wasn't worried, which sort of worried him.

The stop watch clicked as he shot off the starting line. Don didn't remember anything except the stretch of synthetic turf that lay before him.

Spectators watching him run could see the excellent form: Arms in close to body. No extra motion. Good forward lean. But others watching from a closer advantage were left with a few more impressions. The man holding the watch heard it the moment the first stride was completed.

Pflit. Pflit. Pflit.

Scouts and coaches standing along the track heard it as the small guy from Chadron State streaked by them.

Pflit. Pflit. Pflit.

"What the heck was that noise?" a New York Jets scout asked a Raiders official standing next to him.

Moments later, after Beebe crossed the finish line, a Kansas City scout stared at his stop watch, then he glanced down at Don's shoes, where the tread was now so loose it was hanging off to the side. He looked at his stop watch again.

4.25 seconds.

Those number matched the time set by Deion Sanders, on this, the slowest turf in the league. It was a record that would not be broken for eighteen years. On this day, though, the scout circled Don's name, and next to his time he jotted down two words: Check again.

"No one can run that fast," the Kansas City man mumbled, "especially in those goofy shoes."

CHAPTER 16 – Making Believers

As Don quickly found out, run a forty in less than 4.3 and they will come. Even before he returned home from the Combine, those same NFL scouts who couldn't pronounce Chadron, much less find it on a map, were suddenly appearing on the rickety steps of Don Beebe's front porch. Waiting as Beebe pulled up in the car were two burly visitors, one featuring the Raiders' logo on his cap and breast pocket; the other wearing Green Bay's.

"Mr. Beebe, you created a bit of a stir back there in Indianapolis," said Kent McCloughan, a former two-time Pro Bowl cornerback with the Oakland Raiders, who was now working for the Los Angeles team.

"A stir" was putting it mildly. To Diana and Don, it seemed in those days and weeks following the Combine that the phone never stopped ringing, with teams scheduling visits to tiny Chadron every day. Sometimes they even arrived back to back. In the next two weeks, twenty-six teams — all except the Broncos and his own Chicago Bears — came calling, stop watches in hand, to see if what had happened in Indianapolis was an aberration or if this kid really was as fast as proclaimed.

As Combine scout Bill Giles had discovered earlier, it was no easy task getting to Chadron, and he lived in Nebraska. Out-of-state visitors first had to fly in to Denver, then take a 727 to Rapid City, then drive another two hours on a two-lane highway to get to the college.

"I thought you had to have people to have police cars," grunted former quarterback and now Atlanta Falcons coordinator June Jones, after he got busted for going 85 mph on that isolated stretch of highway.

Jones, like all the NFL officials who found their way to Chadron, drove into town skeptical. They knew Beebe was fast, but it just didn't seem possible someone with that kind of speed — Deion Sanders speed, no less — could come out of a place like this. Beebe and Coach Smith were used to hearing the doubt in everyone's voice, which only fueled Don's competitiveness.

"What if I promise to run a 4.2 for you," he told a cocky New York Jets scout who seemed more annoyed than the rest of the NFL lookouts about this inconvenient trip to Chadron.

"Kid, if you can run a 4.3, I'll send Rich Kotite, our head coach, out here to see for himself," the scout replied with a smirk.

Smith made no comment as he listened to the interchange. Then he tried to hide his own smile as the scout stared bug-eyed at his watch after Don ran for him. The man had two clocks on Beebe. One read 4.21; the other, 4.22. "So I guess you'll be sending Kotite out here to see me?" Don inquired.

"He'll be here," the once skeptical scout promised. And Kotite did come. Not only did he put the clock on Don again in the forty — by now, the stop watches were making believers out of all reluctant visitors — Kotite wanted to watch him run a few pass routes. Having speed was important. But a wide receiver has to catch the ball, too.

The problem was, Steward Perez wasn't anywhere around to quarterback for Beebe. And since Kotite or Smith couldn't throw the patterns, that meant the only one left to do the honors was brother Dan, who was a pretty fine basketball player but couldn't toss a football any better than he could as a seven-year-old in the back yard of their Sugar Grove home.

"You gotta be kidding me, right?" Dan said when Coach Smith told him to warm up. "You've obviously never seen me throw or you wouldn't even ask."

Don wasn't too thrilled with the idea, either. This was an important moment. A pro-football head coach had come all this way to see him catch passes, and it wasn't going to help his cause if the ball couldn't get anywhere close to him.

"Bad idea," he moaned as he and his brother took their positions on the field. "You can't throw to save your life. When you do finally get something into the air, it's a lame duck."

A wobbly football is hard enough to catch, but it's a nightmare when thrown low and off target. But options were limited, so Dan figured he might as well give it his best shot. And when that first toss went into the air, no one was more surprised than the impromptu QB that it was a perfect spiral, fast and tight and landing right in the arms of his big brother halfway down the field. So was the next one. And the next one. And the one after that.

"Thank you, God," Don mumbled as he walked off the field. As far as miracles are concerned, turning Dan into a quarterback was up there with the whole water and wine transformation.

Kotite was impressed, too, but not with the Beebe throwing the ball. "This kid's legit," he told Smith after he clocked Don at 4.3 in the forty. "Looks like the trip out to this God-forsaken place was worth it."

A few of the teams didn't bother making the trek, opting instead to fly Beebe to them. When he got to Washington, D.C., for a personal tryout with the Redskins, he was put through even more tests, including one looking for abilities he'd mastered in kindergarten. At one station, Beebe couldn't help but smile when the tester, sitting at a table containing a small collection of children's wooden blocks, asked the six-three prospect being quizzed right before Don to build something higher than it was wide.

The athlete looked puzzled. "You mean higher, like height?" he asked. "I can't tell you any more than that," the tester said.

At first, Don was amused watching the other athlete struggle to complete the task; then he felt sorry for the guy, especially when he walked away mumbling in confusion. When Beebe sat down at the same table, he was dead serious. "Please," he told the official, "whatever you do, don't ask me to build something taller than it is wide. That's insulting."

"Sorry," she shrugged. "That's what I've got to ask."

Don stacked one block on top of another. "Done," he said, clapping his hands together in mock victory.

But he wasn't done with the litany of tests as scouts continued their march to Chadron. Among them was Nick Nicolau, receivers coach for the Buffalo Bills, who had Beebe high on the team's wish list even before sending the Buffalo rep out to Nebraska. Nicolau had not seen Beebe run in Indianapolis, so the kid was pretty much a mystery to him before he arrived in Nebraska.

"What kind of time has he been running?" he asked Smith. The Chadron coach knew if he told the truth, Nicolau wouldn't believe him. "Four point three," he said, shaving a tenth of a second off the time recorded by the Jets scout.

"You got to be kidding me," retorted Nicolau. "If he runs a 4.3, I'll pack him in my suitcase and take him back to New York today."

The Bills coach watched Beebe warm up. Five minutes later, the kid was done. "Takes most guys a good twenty minutes to stretch," he said to Smith.

The Chadron coach shrugged. "What can I say? He's not most guys."

If Nicolau didn't believe that then, he certainly did a few minutes later after he clocked Beebe at 4.25. The Bills coach fought the urge to yell out. Instead, he motioned Beebe back to the starting line. "One more time," Nicolau ordered.

4.28. He kept a poker face. "Once more," he requested.

4.31. He shook his head. "I can't take this back to Buffalo," Nicolau complained to Smith. "No one will believe someone from Chadron State ran this fast. They just won't buy it. Are you sure that distance was measured correctly?"

Without waiting for a response, Nicolau pulled out his tape measure and checked the length himself. "Forty yards exactly," he said, still shaking his head. A half hour later, he was on the phone to his bosses. "I just worked out the guy you're going to want to draft first," he said. "Trust me. He's un-freakin'-believable."

The press seemed to have the same thought. The day after the tests in Indianapolis, ESPN touted Beebe as the surprise of the Combine — a speedster who came out of nowhere and blew away the big-name prospects. A few weeks before the draft, the sports network sent a television crew to Chadron to film "Speed on the Prairie," a special that featured Beebe and another fast prospect from a small college, Jeff Query from Millikin University in Illinois.

So much was happening so quickly, the little Nebraska college could hardly keep up with all the excitement. Each week The Chadron Record, along with the school's newspaper, would report on which NFL teams were coming to town to see their biggest star. Don and Coach Smith were quoted frequently and, for the most part, accurately. And everywhere Beebe went, he was greeted, sometimes even stalked, like an A-list Hollywood celeb on Oscar's big night.

"Pinch me, babe," said Don the night before Draft Day. "In fact, pinch me a couple times. I don't want to wake up and find out it's time to hang aluminum siding."

Diana hugged her husband closely. "You're going to be playing in the NFL, Don," she said, acutely aware of how foreign those words sounded. "At least you won't have to worry anymore about falling off ladders."

CHAPTER 17 – Getting the Call

Don awoke just as the western Nebraska sun made its glorious debut.

It was April 22, 1989, and Diana was still slumbering beside him on the living room's pullout couch. In just a few hours, the NFL draft would begin broadcasting live on ESPN to millions of football fans. If you went by all the scouting reports that had been circulating the past thirty-six hours, Don would probably go somewhere in Round 2 or Round 3. Maybe to the Jets, who had shown the most interest in him. Maybe to Kansas City, who had sent former All-Pro Otis Taylor to work out with him. Then again, the Buffalo Bills, along with the Raiders, Tampa Bay and San Francisco hadn't been shy about letting him know they were interested.

The draft party planned for Morehead Street was still hours away, but already the small house was filling up, with Mom and Dad Beebe sleeping in the only bedroom and two of his sisters camping out with the newlyweds in their cramped living room.

Don was surprised he'd slept so well. Despite the media hype and the steady stream of NFL officials who came rolling into town, he was as calm as he'd been the day he walked into that hotel in Indianapolis. He'd finally secured an agent a few days earlier, a man from California suggested to him by Kay Erickson, whose family owned the Minnesota cabin used by the Beebes all those vacations ago.

"He's an honest, decent man — the kind of agent who isn't going to be lining you up with a string of nitwit girls," she told him. "You can trust him like family, and that's what you need, more than anything."

Bob LaMonte represented a few athletes in California and had never heard of Beebe or Chadron State when Don first contacted him. But after talking to a string of scouts, the affable agent who was known for his integrity and easy grin, realized this kid from the Midwest was something remarkable, especially when he was assured the 4.2 was no exaggeration.

"Don't be disappointed if you go a little lower than Round 2 or Round 3," he told Don in one of his many phone calls the previous evening. "These things are always kind of hard to call."

Don wasn't worried. He was just happy his family and friends would be here to celebrate. His mom had gone to Chadron's very best bakery — OK, so it was the town's only bakery — to buy a humongous round chocolate cake decorated with NFL lettering. She'd also picked up construction paper at a craft store and made twenty-eight flags — each representing a team — and planted them atop the icing. There was plenty of cold cuts, potato salad and desserts in the fridge, too, enough to feed a small army. And soon the entire home, as crowded as it was now, would be rocking with even more well-wishers.

Don rolled out of bed so as not to awaken Diana, and made his way to the bathroom that was blessedly unoccupied. He stared at his reflection in the mirror as he grabbed his toothbrush and razor. Was this the face of an NFL football player or an aluminum siding man? He grinned at the reflection staring back at him. Beebe still had a hard time believing all this was taking place, yet he also knew it was exactly what should be happening because he had followed a calling he'd first pronounced in that small Aurora church when he was just a little kid.

"I may not know exactly what's going to happen today, Lord. But I know whatever it is, you are in control."

With the house still slumbering, he threw on a pair of jeans left by the side of his makeshift bed and stepped outside. He could smell the lilacs near his front porch. He sat on the crumbling step and thought about the many different roads his life could have taken. Don enjoyed the accolades. He enjoyed the competition. And if he didn't exactly enjoy the pressure he'd been under this past year, he certainly tried to make it work for him. But he was also convinced all the blessings raining down on him now were for a reason that went beyond a locker room or football field.

The front door creaked, and Don looked into his father's face. "Pretty big day for you, isn't it?" the older man said as he took a seat next to his son. "But I know you're ready for it."

Don placed his hand on his dad's shoulder. He noticed his father's own strong hands —still surprisingly soft after decades of manual labor. Don had been fortunate to play under some great coaches so far, but it was this man sitting here, now brushing away some piece of imaginary dirt on his jeans, who had taught him the most about being a winner. This day would not have come if his dad hadn't sacrificed for him and, yes, pushed him. If not for his dad's support, he might have quit football a half-dozen times. If not for his dad's example, he might not have seen a path to the Lord or learned the value of persistence. Somewhere along the way, his father had taught him not just how to be a man, but how to be a good man. There is a difference.

"I just want you to know I couldn't be more proud of you," Don Beebe Sr. said. "And I hope I've been the kind of father to you that I needed when I was growing up."

Don didn't say anything. He knew his father's childhood hadn't been the best, but the older man rarely talked about it.

"I could have been a good athlete," Don Sr. said, his eyes staring straight ahead, brow furrowed slightly. "Probably not as good as you. I was fast, though. No idea how fast. But in gym class I'd beat all the other guys whenever we ran races. Left 'em in the dust, actually."

Don grinned. "Seriously, Dad? You were that fast, huh?"

"His dad nodded. "Fast enough the teacher noticed. He was the track coach and he wanted me to go out for the team. He begged me … more than a few times. But I always told him no."

Don Sr. looked down and shook his head. "I remember going home and telling my dad about the track team. He told me not to waste my time. It would take away from working after school. And I guess it would have."

"Did you want to go out?" Don asked. "Were you mad your dad wouldn't let you?"

"It wasn't like he ordered me not to," Don Sr. replied. "He just made it perfectly clear to me I'd be wasting my time. He didn't give me any guidance or encouragement to try other things."

"So what did you do in high school?"

"I smoked cigarettes. I did some drag racing. Loved those flathead V8s. Guess I'm sort of like Ponyboy from 'The Outsiders.' I was a greaser. Hung around on street corners and thought I was one tough son of a gun."

Don laughed. "You sounded kinda cool, Dad?"

"Not at all. I had absolutely no purpose. No goals. No direction. College was never mentioned. It was not an option, even if I would have studied and made decent grades."

"So what happened? When did it all start coming together for you."

"I was 24. Dating your mother, who was a wonderful woman. Beautiful. Kind. I had a couple of friends who invited me to come with them to a revival at Soul Harbor Church. Not even sure why I went. It was God's plan, for sure. He knew I was searching. He knew my heart was ready for direction."

Don was intrigued. "Were you saved that first night?"

Don Sr. nodded. "I realized then that I had to stop using my lousy childhood as an excuse. Sure I would have wanted a better dad, even if I didn't know it at the time. But it hit me that night that I had control of my future. That there was a higher power who could give me the direction I didn't even know I craved so badly. I fell to my knees and accepted the Lord on that day."

He raised his eyes to look at his son. "From that moment on, Donny, I vowed to change the legacy of the Beebe name."

Don felt a lump form in his throat. He was suddenly consumed with newfound love and respect for this man who had been there for him as long as he could remember.

"My faith is what drives me, Don. It keeps me focused. It is unshakable. If someone told me I had to die a martyr's death for the Lord, I would ask 'Where's the bullet?' You've got that same faith, Son. I'm proud of all you've accomplished on the football field. But mostly I'm proud because you've got that same faith."

Don swiped at his eyes. He saw his father do the same.

"I don't know what's gonna happen today," he told his dad. "But I promise you, if God sees fit to give me a career in the NFL, I'll use that opportunity to do his work."

The elder Beebe suddenly took an interest in the worn front porch. "You got a board loose here," he said, struggling to keep emotion from his voice. "Think you can round me up a hammer and a few nails to take care of this before everyone gets here?"

It took longer to locate the tools than it did to complete the fix-it job. Don's dad spent the next couple of hours scouring the home for other tasks that would keep him productive and occupied. By mid-morning, the house was offering standing-room-only accommodations.

Don's friend Jim Angell, grinning like a kid at Christmas and carrying a slow cooker filled with Italian beef, arrived not long after the Beebe women had laid out the food on the kitchen counters and small table. His brother Dave, who had been bunking with Dan in the dorm, rumbled into the driveway around 10 a.m. They claimed prime positions in front of the twenty-inch TV, even though the coverage would not begin until noon. By then, more than two dozen people, including friends and Chadron coaches and players, were vying for the last good viewing spots.

The excitement was infectious: The women chattered and the men threw NFL stats around like farmers sowing spring wheat. But a hush settled over the room when the draft finally kicked off. Paul Tagliabue would step to the microphone and, one by one, announce the names of players surely destined to lead their teams to the playoff promised land.

First to go was the UCLA quarterback, Troy Aikman, picked up by the Dallas Cowboys after a 3-13 finish in 1988, Tom Landry's last season as head coach. Next was the jinxed Sports Illustrated cover boy, offensive lineman Tony Mandarich, who proudly donned his new Green Bay Packers hat. Then Detroit nabbed Barry Sanders, with Kansas City taking Derrick Thomas; and the flashy Deion Sanders going to the Atlanta Falcons. And so Round 1 went — one player after another getting the call that would change their lives — until Keith DeLong was picked up by San Francisco.

Spirits in the little house on Morehead remained high. Each time the phone rang, half the people in the room jumped. Could this be the call? But it was always from one of dozens of well-wishers who seemed awfully appreciative they'd even been able to get through on the busy phone. Then, as Round 2 commenced, with the Cowboys picking up Steve Wisniewski first and Detroit naming John Ford, an air of anxiousness settled over the room.

The anxiety only grew as the afternoon wore on. Round 3 began with Mark Stepnoski going to Dallas and Matt Brock to Green Bay. At 5:00 p.m. when the televised coverage stopped, still near the top of Round 3, Don could sense the letdown. But no one said anything for fear of sounding the alarm. "It's really not that big of a deal," Don tried to reassure his guests. "We'll find out tomorrow."

It turned out he was only half-right. Seven minutes after five, as the hungriest of his visitors were piling on more Italian beef and the conversations were growing louder again, the phone rang.

No one heard it at first. Don, in the middle of a mouthful of potato salad, eventually noticed the jangling. He dropped his plate so he could grab the receiver, expecting yet another Sugar Grove supporter on the other end. He didn't have time to swallow his food before saying, "Hello?"

"Is this Don Beebe?"

He almost choked on potato salad. "Yes, sir, it is."

"Well, Don, I'm calling to inform you the Buffalo Bills have chosen you as their first pick in the draft, in the third round, the eighty-second pick overall. Congratulations, Son. You are now a Buffalo Bill."

The words had yet to sink in. But the reply was polite and automatic. "Thank you, sir. I'm very happy to be part of your organization."

It was exactly what the crowd, silenced as they listened to one half of this phone conversation, had been waiting for. The house erupted in shrieks, cheers and applause. Diana hugged her mother-in-law, who hugged her daughters who hugged their brothers who both grabbed their dad's hand and shook it so hard, his glasses rattled on the end of his nose.

106

Then came the questions: Who was on the other end of the phone? Was it a coach? His agent? Did Don get drafted? Who would Don be playing for?

Still in conversation with an unfamiliar voice, Don was only vaguely aware of what his family and friends were asking. Barb couldn't wait. She held up one of her construction-paper flags representing the Jets. Don, still on the phone, shook his head. His father held up the Tampa Bay flag. No, again. His sister held up the Raiders flag. Same response. Kansas City?

On the other end of the line, Don was told he needed to make flight arrangements as soon as possible to New York. He was given the name of a secretary to contact. Don wrote her name — N-I-N-A — on a sheet of paper.

Diana read the scrawl. "The Niners!" she called out to her guests. "It's the San Francisco 49ers!"

The cheer that erupted was so boisterous, Coach Smith, who was only now arriving, heard it from two blocks away. By this time, Don was talking to Bills head Coach Marv Levy.

"You were the guy we wanted," he assured Beebe. "And because of a few trades we had, we didn't have a pick until the third round. We were absolutely thrilled that you were still there. Welcome to a proud and successful football franchise."

Buffalo was indeed an enviable place to land. The organization was one of the strongest up-and-coming teams in the AFC, with a dynamic quarterback named Jim Kelly who many considered the best in the league. Diana had been hoping Don would get tagged by a team from a less frigid state — Tampa Bay, after all, had shown as much interest as anyone. But in the end, it really didn't matter if she would still be wearing her parka for much of the year. Knowing how much her husband had dreamed of this moment warmed her from the tip of her head to the bottom of her feet.

Later, after most of the guests had left and she was cleaning up crunched soda cans, she remembered their first date, when they shared that pepperoni pizza and Coke, and Don announced with all the confidence of a sixteen-year-old that he was going to do something special in sports.

As exhaustion finally won out over the adrenalin rush of the last twenty-four hours, she closed her eyes and prayed that God would not change the heart of this wonderful young man she so deeply loved.

"No matter how successful or how long his career is in the NFL, keep him in your graces," she whispered. "And please, please Lord, protect him from all those players who are a whole lot bigger than he is."

CHAPTER 18 – Doubting the Dream

Don and Diana stepped into the terminal of Buffalo International Airport and were hit by a throng of reporters, photographers and TV crewmen who greeted them like rock band groupies backstage after a concert.

Don could feel his young bride's hand, tucked protectively inside his own, tense up as she took in the media blitz. "Don't worry," he whispered, squeezing her fingers gently. "There's something else going on that's got this many reporters here."

He was right. About the same time the Beebes landed in Buffalo — less than forty-eight hours after the NFL draft party — Alexander Mogilny, a star Russian hockey player, defected to the United States to play for the Buffalo Sabres, attracting journalists from across two continents. With the sports world all aflutter over this international storyline, the Bills' first draft pick was relegated to a below-the-fold headline on sports pages. Which suited Beebe just fine.

Not that there wasn't plenty of curiosity about Buffalo's new what's-his-name wide receiver. After draft day, sports reporters and their editors struggled to find any significant information about this latest hometown celebrity that hadn't been handed to them in press releases from the Bills. Chadron State had been only marginally helpful: The school didn't even have game film of their star receiver because they claimed he was too fast to be caught by their cameras.

Most of the cynical Buffalo journalists scoffed at such hyperbole. Armed with microphones and cameras, they were determined to figure out just what the heck this unexpected No. 1 pick was all about.

"So, Don, is it true you only played two years of college ball?" a balding reporter with the Buffalo Evening News asked, his Bic poised and ready, even as he fumbled with a miniature tape recorder.

"How does it feel, coming to a big city like Buffalo?" asked another journalist, this one a tanned TV personality with a dentistry-enhanced smile.

Don didn't quite know how to respond to some of the more inane questions. No doubt Mr. Shiny Teeth was checking out the clothes Beebe had decided to wear on his "Say Hello to Buffalo" trip: a well-worn dark blue sweatshirt, sleeves slightly frayed at the end, and his best blue jeans, a pair of Levis he'd purchased only a few weeks earlier at the Chadron Wal-Mart.

"After you get to your hotel, make sure you change into a suit," suggested Don's agent, Bob LaMonte, who had met the Beebes at the airport. "You're not a poor college kid anymore, and you want to look sharp at the press conference tomorrow."

"Press conference?" Don croaked. Even repeating the words caused his heart to skip a beat and the palms of his hands to break into a sweat. Beebe was apprehensive — no, make that terrified — of public speaking. Any kind of public speaking. Even getting up in front of his peers in speech class at Kaneland High — the same kids he performed for with spectacular grace under Friday-night football lights — was an ordeal that would keep him up nights. The only way he could get through it without hyperventilating was to pick a subject so familiar to him that it was like talking to his buddies or his kid brothers. "How to Gut a Fish" got him a B-minus in Mrs. Erdmann's English class. And he managed to get a C-plus later that semester for his persuasive speech on why female reporters should not be allowed into a men's locker room for post-game interviews.

Right now, though, he had bigger worries. Don didn't own a suit or a tie. In fact, what he was wearing now was pretty much the best he had. And since there had been no time to go on a shopping junket to Macy's, or Kmart for that matter, LaMonte did what any agent worth his weight in commissions would do: He shook the jacket off his back and put it on his client.

Not a perfect fit, but none of the journalists at the afternoon press conference at Rich Stadium seemed to notice as they peppered the rookie and Marv Levy with questions about this unusual new Bill who could supposedly run with record-breaking speed. Their inquiries, Don figured, were a mixture of humor, curiosity and downright skepticism. But no matter how these media folks approached the interview, all of them were after a good story.

No doubt about it: Don Beebe was a good story.

"We could have gone with a wide receiver from Duke or North Carolina," Levy explained to the media-packed room. "But when we saw that Beebe was still on the board in the third round, when we got to make our first pick, we knew we had to take him. Those who passed him up didn't do their homework."

His audience wasn't so convinced. "But Coach, aren't you taking a big chance on a player from such a small school?" called out a Channel 2 reporter from the third row. "How do you really know how these picks will stack up when the level of competition is so different at a D-I?"

Levy looked at the skinny young man who asked the question and offered him a half-smile. "Son, you're taking your chances no matter who you draft, as you sports folks all know. But as you also may have heard, the one thing Don has is speed. That's undeniable. And it's the same no matter what division he played in. You've got to have speed if you're going to be a wide receiver."

Truth was, Levy knew he was taking a chance drafting Beebe as high as he did. His size was definitely a minus. But he liked what he had seen on the tapes; and John Butler, his director of player personnel, saw something special in the clean-cut kid who could run like nobody's business. The head coach was placing a lot of faith in his staff and in his gut. In fact, Levy hadn't even met Beebe until the night before. He and his wife Fran were dining at Salvatore's Italian Garden in Buffalo when the waiter came up to him and pointed to a young couple sitting at a table across the room.

"That guy right there says you drafted him," the server said. "Is that true, Coach?"

Levy glanced over at the young attractive couple – the pretty blond and her fresh-faced dinner partner dressed in an ill-fitting brown suit jacket. When he walked over and introduced himself, Levy could see the intelligence in the young man's eyes; the genuine excitement in his broad grin. And he knew instantly that this draft pick was a smart choice.

"We didn't know a lot about the kid, but it was all favorable stuff," the coach told the media hounds. "We were very lucky to get him."

When it was Don's turn to address the crowd, he tried not to over-think his remarks. He thanked the Bills for giving him the chance to play in the NFL, and professed his enthusiasm at being in Buffalo with such a great team with such great fans. Standard stuff.

But was he ever thankful when it was over. Although Don had managed to get through the rest of the press conference without stuttering, stammering or passing out, he realized he'd have to at some point deal with his phobia about public speaking. But so much was happening all at once, he wasn't quite sure if the funny feeling in his stomach was the by-product of change occurring at lightning speed; or if he was succumbing to the pressure that he had, up until now, managed to keep at bay.

He was just relieved when that whirlwind Buffalo trip was over and he and Diana could return to Chadron so he could finish up his classes. Twenty-one credit hours short of graduating, Don's thoughts at this point were hardly on a degree in business and marketing. But he promised Diana that when football finally came to an end, he'd return to Chadron to get that diploma.

"I just wish I had a dollar for every time someone patted me on the back and shook my hand today," he joked, as he and Diana began packing up the tiny Morehead Street house that had come to mean so much to them. "Then maybe we could have enough money to get that last electric bill paid off."

Diana laughed. "Don, you still don't get it. We do have enough money now to pay off that bill. And the gas bill. And the money we owe your folks for that one month of rent we had to borrow. And you know what? We've even got enough left over to go to that movie you've been promising me for, oh, let's see, about four months now."

It was a lot to grasp for a young couple so used to pinching pennies. Within a few weeks, they were back in Buffalo, and this time, the top priority was meeting with a Realtor. By the end of their first day of house hunting, the Beebes had signed a six-month lease on a modest townhome — at 1,800 square feet, it was positively palatial compared to their college digs — and had gone shopping for clothes at the mall. With his $110,000 signing bonus and a yearly salary of another $110,000, the newlyweds felt like they had just hit the lottery.

Still, there was a reason Don wanted to rent a modest townhome instead of buying a house. In those rare quiet moments during the days leading up to mini-camp, Don found himself questioning whether he was even good enough to make the team.

Beebe's biggest fear, as he donned his first Bills helmet that third week in May, was getting off the line of scrimmage. As much as he hated to admit it, some of Mr. Shiny Teeth's questions were right on target. The opponents he'd face now were a whole lot bigger than the athletes he'd gone up against in this past. While he could easily out-juke any defensive back's bump-and-run coverage during his days at Chadron State, here the big boys across the line were almost as fast as he was.

And he quickly learned just how much he still had to learn as he lined up on that first day of drills at Rich Stadium.

CHAPTER 19 – Toughening Up

The sky was cloudless, and the air was calm as a convent of nuns during vespers. But Nate Odomes stood on the other side of the scrimmage line, looming over Beebe like a creature from hell.

One of the top five defensive backs in the NFL, the six-foot Pro-Bowler was built like an Army tank with a massive chest and sweat-drenched guns for biceps. And he wasn't smiling.

In fact, Beebe was certain that was a snarl on his face. As Don looked into the other man's eyes, dark as death and staring straight into his soul, he was convinced he was in over his head. Even worse, Odomes knew it, too.

The ball was snapped and before Don even had time to twitch a muscle, the big back delivered a thundering forearm shiver to Beebe's chest.

"UUGH!" Don fell backward, slipped on the soft turf and landed square on his behind. "Stay down there, rookie," Odomes grunted. "You're gonna be there all year anyway."

Don was too stunned to feel much of anything, but only for a moment. Then a wave of humiliation washed over him. He wanted to dig a hole through the turf so he could crawl into it. Instead, he jumped up to finish his routes, more embarrassed than he'd ever been on a football field. And one thought raced through his mind: *Well, Donny, you're not in Chadron anymore.*

After the mini-camp broke, Beebe knew he had his work cut out for him. For the next three months, he accelerated his fitness routine and followed a strict protein-rich diet, both of which put him in the best shape of his life. Still, Don recognized his Achilles heel. He was quick and he was determined. But he wasn't prepared to play with the big boys of the NFL. As hard as he hit the weights, he'd received no specialized training in coming off the line of scrimmage. That meant he reported to the 1989 Bills summer camp in August bulkier,   but just as naïve as when Odomes shoved him to the ground a few months earlier.

As he walked onto the practice field, for a brief moment he fantasized about turning tail and heading back to his apartment. He could quickly pack his bags, and he and Diana could jump on the next plane to Chicago where he wouldn't have to worry about big angry machines in cleats taking him down.

He knew whatever he lacked in technique, he more than made up for in God-given determination. He just wasn't convinced persistence alone would cut it in the NFL.

Beebe swiped at the beads of sweat dotting his brow. As the receivers formed one line that would take on the backs in the opposite line, he scanned the landscape to check out who he'd be matched against.

Don was standing fourth in line. So was Odomes, on the other side of the line.

Beebe groaned. The last thing he was going to do was let Nate the Great perform an encore. After all, how many times can a man be knocked down and still call himself a man? All in the name of self-preservation, Beebe took a knee, grabbed the laces of his right cleat and pretended to tie his shoe, just long enough for a couple of receivers to go ahead of him in the line. Then, for good measure, he took off his helmet and began adjusting the strap, allowing yet a couple more teammates to walk around him.

It worked like a charm and he kept up the calculated sidesteps for the remainder of the drills. Not that anyone else seemed to notice. Except for one.

"Hey, Rookie," Odomes called out as he headed to the shower after practice. "Nice defense."

* * *

Don's main focus in those couple of weeks before reporting to camp was figuring out a way to keep from getting shamed again by the likes of Nate Odomes. "You need a strong dose of quickness and confidence, Beebs," said Scott Berchtold, the marketing director and team spokesman for the Bills, when Don finally confessed his concerns. "And I've got the guy to provide both."

His name was Gary Canstanza, who had earned the title of soke in the martial arts world for mastering a move called the "one-inch punch." And the first time Don walked into his dojo, he knew this man was for real. Canstanza was short, stout and rock-hard. Don quickly found out just how hard when the teacher challenged the pupil to try to push him down. Beebe, as strong as he was after a summer of intense workouts, couldn't budge the man, no matter how he tried.

"Make no mistake about it," Canstanza told Don on that first session together. "As an NFL player, you are engaged in hand-to-hand combat every game. And your job is to keep the defensive back's hands off you. You must take him out each time there is contact."

He offered to show Don the move that Bruce Lee made famous back in 1964. "Here, take this clipboard and hold it against your chest," Canstanza ordered. "It's to protect your sternum from breaking when I hit you."

"You're gonna hit me that hard?" Don squawked, now a tad nervous at what was about to come at him.

"Don't worry," Canstanza assured his pupil. "If you do just what I tell you, you should be OK."

Should be?

Canstanza stood in front of Beebe, his fist centimeters from Don's chest. The trainer was so close, Don could feel his breath and count the number of crinkles around his eyes. "I'm going to give you a good pop, so brace yourself," Canstanza warned. "And whatever you do, keep that clipboard against your body."

Beebe knew a thing or two about intensity, but this guy was something else. Suddenly, Canstanza's pupils seemed to turn a shade darker. He closed his eyes and inhaled deeply. He released the breath and inhaled again. His facial muscles tightened. Release. Silence. The ten seconds that followed felt more like twenty.

"AYIEEEEEEEE!"

The soke's right hand exploded, popping Beebe so hard in the chest he flew into the padded wall six feet away. Don had no time to react. He fell to the floor. He sat there for a moment, stunned. He blinked, shook his head and slowly rose to his feet. The clipboard, which had gone flying on impact, lay on the floor a couple feet away. Don was aware of pressure on his chest where the blow had landed. Otherwise, he felt nothing but amazement.

"Bro," he laughed, shaking his head in disbelief. "You've got to teach me how to do that!"

Twice a week for the entire six-month off-season, Don met with the soke at his Buffalo training center. And in that time, Don Beebe morphed into a different athlete.

"You can't create speed," Canstanza told his pupil, "unless you are relaxed. And you can't play without attitude. When you face Nate

118

Odomes, you have to know you can take him out. Him, or anyone else who gets in your way.

"No matter what the odds," he said, "you can win the battle."

Beebe's final exam came in May 1990 at the Bills mini-camp. In the first one-on-one between defensive backs and wide receivers, he was about to find out if all those months of training had paid off.

Lining up to run his first route, Don watched as Kirby Jackson, the other starting cornerback, stepped up to guard Beebe.

"No," Don told him. He looked at Odomes. "Nate, you and me. Let's go."

The big man's face reflected his surprise. It was out of character to call anyone out like that at a practice. Certainly not Nate Odomes. But this day was different.

The question mark had to be addressed. Don had to know right then and there if he had what it took. Beebe turned to Jim Kelly. He held up his left hand and made a fist, the sign that he was going deep.

Nate knew what that signal meant, as well. Don didn't care. In fact, he hoped the Pro-Bowler knew exactly where he was going. Beebe was going to beat his teammate deep, and there was nothing Odomes could do about it.

The ball was snapped. Beebe's arm shot out, delivering a quick chop to Odomes' forearm and knocking it off Don's shoulder pads. The move cost Nate his balance just enough for Don to blow by him. He ran toward the end zone and Kelly lofted the ball in his direction.

It was an easy score, and as Beebe threw the ball to the ground, he lifted his head to the sky. He was pumped. Vindicated. He had just beaten one of the top five backs in the National Football League. Now, for the first time, he knew he belonged.

CHAPTER 20 – Scoring in Prime Time

Despite his success on the line of scrimmage and his intense workouts that resulted in a bigger, quicker, stronger body, Beebe's rookie year was marred by injury. Three days into camp, he tore his left hamstring, and injured it again a few weeks later. Still, even with those setbacks and his inexperience, he managed to make a name for himself early on in the season. And he did so in flamboyant fashion.

The match-up was with the Houston Oilers. The Bills' first away game would be nationally televised on a rare Saturday afternoon, but Don wasn't sure if he'd even get into the game.

In the NFL, most coaches use a two-wide-receiver set, and on passing downs, a third receiver goes on the field to shake things up. At the beginning of the season, Beebe was listed behind Andre Reed, Chris Burkett and Flip Johnson. That meant in the first two games, both of them at home in Rich Stadium, he didn't get off the sideline. But Kelly was impressed with the rookie's attitude, on and off the field. He'd noticed Beebe's toughness in practice and how quickly he picked up the routes. And the rookie's speed – to a quarterback looking for a wide receiver to blow past those pesky defensive backs – was a thing of beauty. Kelly's motive for approaching Levy the first day of practice after the second game was purely selfish: He wanted the best matchup possible.

"We need to get Beebe in the game," he told the coach. "I want to throw it to him deep to open it up for Andre to spread the defense."

The next day, Levy summoned Burkett to his office and told him to clean out his locker. Just like that, Beebe was the third receiver on the team.

Don felt bad for the affable Burkett, but he also knew there was a reason sportscasters joked that the NFL stood for "Not For Long." There was little time for sentiment in the dog-eat-dog world of professional football.

When he called his family in Sugar Grove, he tried to play it cool. "You better be watching the game in Houston on Saturday afternoon," he told his mom. "I don't know how much I'll get the ball. But look for me on the field 'cause I'm gonna be in there on every third down."

The news spread through town like Barb's oatmeal pancake batter on a hot griddle. And on game day, after making a big family breakfast – no flapjacks but plenty of eggs and bacon – she stayed in the kitchen long enough to also conjure up a big pot of Italian beef, potato salads and desserts that would feed the two dozen people planning to cram into the Beebe home for this must-see TV.

Don slept like a baby in his Hyatt room in downtown Houston the night before the game. When he was prepared — and boy, was he prepared for this day — he always managed to catch plenty of shut-eye. Even breakfast went down with relative ease; egg whites, a banana, wheat toast with peanut butter. It was standard fare for players the morning before a game. Still, there was nothing standard about this day, and that fact hit him the moment he stepped onto the field of the Astrodome.

All his dreams and a whole lot of his prayers were focused on this moment . Here he was on national TV. In an NFL uniform. Under the Astrodome.

The locker room was smaller than most NFL dressing rooms, more like a high school's. But it was a hub of activity as the team fell into its pre-game rituals. Don arrived two hours before kickoff. He sat on the wood bench and pulled out his well-thumbed playbook. He'd been reading it almost nonstop for the last four days, but he wanted to review it one more time. He tried to drown out any exterior noise as he scanned the pages to make sure each route was etched into his brain.

After fifteen minutes, Beebe closed the book and took a deep breath. He pulled out his headphones, and soon Kenny G's soothing notes filled his head. He opened his Bible and began reading silently. The verses, the soothing music, he hoped, would help him stay calm, focused.

As the locker room filled, the noise seemed to subside. Players were quiet, pacing or sitting in stone silence. Like Beebe, they were deep in their own thoughts, their own music. An hour before kickoff, Bud Carpenter walked over to Don, the trainer's large hands holding a roll of white tape. "Let's get you wrapped, Beebs," he said. "This is your day."

Don was convinced he was as prepared as he could possibly be. But even that knowledge could not keep all doubts at bay. It was all about performing. He had to go out there today and do the job, not so much for the media or even his family watching at home. He had to prove to the other guys on the team he was the real deal. He had to show the coaches, especially those who pushed so hard to make him their first pick, he was worth the risk. Despite his readiness, he felt his chest tighten with the realization so much was riding on these next four quarters.

After the trainer finished wrapping Beebe's ankles and wrists, Don, still dressed in gray shorts and a T-shirt, pulled off his headphones. He picked up a loose ball and walked through the tunnel, onto the field. The seats were mostly vacant, with only a few stadium workers scuttling about as they put final touches on the field.

Empty or not, he felt the rush. This was the Astrodome: the first covered sports stadium, once billed as the Eighth Wonder of the World.

Where Judy Garland performed the day it opened back in 1965. Where Nolan Ryan pitched no-hitters and Elvis began a comeback tour. And now here he was, on this same stage.

Scott Berchtold caught up with the rookie and threw his right arm across Don's shoulders. "Been looking for you, Beebs," said the marketing director, who had joined the Bills the same month Beebe arrived in camp. "Just want to say good luck. I know you'll make us all proud."

Beebe strolled around the field for a few more minutes. He walked over to the sidelines and sat on the bench. He stared at the sixty thousand seats that surrounded him. More than a few rows were beginning to fill with early arrivals.

He wondered what would happen today. Would the butterflies go away once he was in the game? Would he get the ball thrown to him enough to make a difference? Would he score a touchdown? Would he be the hero? Would he embarrass himself in front of a national audience?

The questions rolled through Don's head like waves on a tumultuous sea. Soon enough he'd have the answers to them all.

Don returned to the locker room and began strapping on his pads. He stepped into his game pants. He pulled his jersey over his chest. Player chatter picked up but it wasn't loud enough to cover the crowd noise that permeated the walls. The Astrodome was filling up. He picked up his helmet and stared at the top of it.

There wasn't a whole lot left to do but pray. When he was through, he lifted his head and looked into the friendly face of Nick Nicolau, the receivers coach. "You ready to rock 'n' roll, Beebs?"

Marv Levy motioned for the team to gather around him. Don took his spot near the front of the huddle and bowed his head as the coach led the athletes in the "Our Father." For the veteran leader, it was all about being ready to go into battle, mentally, physically, and yes, even spiritually. A national television audience was ready to see what the Bills were made of, Levy told his team. Don't let the crowd take them out of the game, especially in the first quarter.

The coach caught Beebe's eyes. "You've prepared your entire life for this moment," he assured the rookie. "I wouldn't put you out there if I didn't think you were ready."

Don nodded his appreciation, as a roar went up from outside the room. The Houston Oilers were taking the field. A few minutes later, he and the Bills stormed through the same tunnel.

The reception was much cooler for the visitors as they spilled onto the turf. But Beebe didn't notice. It took a half second for his eyes to adjust to the bright lights and the flashing cameras. He looked around the stadium again — only now, every seat was filled. The air crackled with anticipation and Wild Cherry's "Play That Funky Music." Was it his imagination, or could he actually smell the hot dogs even from down here on the field? It reminded him of the brats from the concession stand at Kaneland High School.

Right now thousands of fans were sitting in the sixty-dollar seats that surrounded him, with millions more watching from their couches or sprawled in recliners as they drank beer and fiddled with TV remotes. But the fans first in his mind were in Sugar Grove, all of whom whooped and whistled when, just minutes after kickoff, No. 82 finally trotted onto the field.

Barb became so excited, she dropped a plate of brownies; and sister Beth let out a shriek loud enough to wake the baby who had been napping in the bedroom down the hall.

"Quiet down, everyone, they're talking about Donny!" ordered Jeff Still, Beebe's old childhood buddy. Still sporting a grin as wide as his shoulders, Jeff was now a popular teacher at a middle school and an assistant football coach at Waubonsie Valley High School, both in Aurora. He and his brother had remained close friends with the Beebe boys, even as their paths took off in different directions.

"We're going to get our first look at the Bills' No. 1 draft pick," NBC sports commentator Bob Trumpy told his audience. "No doubt they want to take advantage of Beebe's impressive speed. So look for Kelly to throw it deep."

The man knew what he was talking about. With a third and six, the Bills had the ball on their own 37-yard line when the franchise quarterback ordered the rookie to run a deep fly. Beebe lined up across from the Oiler's Cris Dishman, a second-year pro swift enough to also have run track for the Purdue Boilermakers. Even beneath the helmet, Beebe could see Dishman's eyes sizzle as he sized up his new opponent.

The defensive back nodded his head and grinned at Don. "White Boy," he cooed, "let's see that speed everyone's talking about."

He didn't have to wait long. On the next play, Kelly held on to the ball himself and ran it eight yards for a first down. Back in the huddle, the QB spat out his new orders. "We're going to do a post, corner route. Spread right. They're running past the corner. Beebs: If he's pressing you, I'm throwing it to you, so run deep."

Beebe swallowed. His first thought was, *Oh, my gosh, don't throw it to me.* That was followed by, *Oh my gosh, throw it to me.* Which was followed by, *Oh my gosh, PLEASE don't throw it to me.*

Don wasn't quite sure what prayer was going through his mind when Kelly snapped the ball. Beebe cut quickly to his right, whipped past Dishman and raced down the right side of the field. He crossed the fifty, then past the Oilers' forty. Then the thirty. Forty yards down field, he glanced back. Kelly was deep in the pocket, his feet planted firmly on the

Oiler's 28-yard-line and looking Beebe's way. The quarterback's right arm pulled back, and in the flash of a camera, the ball launched, missile-like, into the air.

Oh my gosh, Beebe thought, *he threw it to me!* Which meant he had to catch it. Only problem was, Don wasn't exactly sure where the ball was. Because it was sailing so high — more like a punt — Beebe lost sight of it in the white stadium lights. The good news? There was no time to panic. With Dishman trailing him by a mere five yards, Don concentrated on keeping his stride, even as he stuck out his hand, praying he knew the general vicinity of the ball.

He felt a surge of adrenalin as flesh touched leather. Snatching the ball from the air at the twenty-five-yard line, Beebe tipped his feet to stay in bounds – and felt Dishman's desperate grab to the back of his jersey. There was a sharp pull. Then nothing. He turned on the jets.

Six seconds later, he trotted into the end zone, scoring a sixty-three-yard touchdown the first time he touched a ball in a professional football game. And the rookie had no idea what he was supposed to do next. So he skipped around the end zone like a little girl — until Andre ran up on his left and tackled him to the turf.

Lying under the Bills' star receiver, Beebe's first thought was how cool this must be for his family. Sure enough, in Sugar Grove, the eruption was even louder than those Draft Day cheers in Chadron a mere six months earlier. In Frank Reich's home in Buffalo, his wife Linda and Diana hugged each other and jumped up and down as tears spilled onto Diana's cheeks.

Back in Houston, a sheepish Oilers DB approached Don as he walked off the field.

"Whadaya know?" he said. "I guess the white boy can run."

126

CHAPTER 21 – Breaking the News

That Saturday afternoon touchdown, replayed often on prime-time TV, was instrumental in the Bills' 47-41 overtime win over the Oilers. It wasn't until later along the sidelines of the Houston game that Don realized Cris Dishman had yanked from his jersey the middle E of Beebe's name. "You were so dang fast, Beebs," Kelly joked, "the letters just flew off your shirt."

Later that week, that missing letter would become the focus of a 97 Rock contest, as the radio station DJ asked his listeners to please find Don's E and bring it to the next game. Thousands of fans showed up at Rich Stadium the following week, with every kind of E imaginable. A pipefitter won the contest, for his nine-foot letter made out of corrugated steel. Buffalo, it seemed, finally knew who the little receiver from Chadron State was. And they eventually came to realize that, unlike many of his colleagues in the NFL, this rookie with the blazing speed was no head case.

Except in one game, that is, when his head's case became a topic of concern to sports fans around the country.

Because he reinjured his hamstring a few weeks after the Oilers' shootout, Beebe was sidelined four long weeks his rookie year. But he earned himself another highlight video in the Bills' last game of the season, a playoff game against Cleveland on January 6, 1990. Late in the second quarter, Beebe got upended. As his head torpedoed into the ground, a loud groan erupted through the stadium. Fans and foes alike knew instantly what a dangerous hit he just took.

Along the sidelines, players and coaches caught their breath as they watched this human Pogo. More than one thought the worst, as Beebe lay motionless on the ground. But he popped back up, with only a severe sprain to his neck. And even that wasn't enough to keep him off the field, despite recommendations from the team doctor and trainers that he rest his injury for at least forty-eight hours.

"I'm not sitting out," Don told Bud Carpenter after the trainer examined him in the locker room. "I've missed too many games already this season, and as long as it's just a sprain, I can play."

In the final minutes, the Bills trailed by six points and needed a touchdown to keep their playoff hopes alive. On fourth and ten, Don, showing no fear despite the earlier mishap, flew over the middle, and Kelly hit him with a rocket for a first down.

"I tell you what," Nicolau said to the trainer as Don jogged off the field. "Beebe may not be the biggest guy out there, but he might just be the toughest."

The drive ultimately fell short, ending the Bills season and Don's roller coaster of a rookie year. His stats included seventeen catches for more than three hundred yards. And, if nothing else, that first year proved to a whole lot of naysayers that the little player from Chadron State could play on Sunday afternoons.

As the 1990 season kicked off, Don felt his confidence grow. "God willing," he told Diana, "if I can just stay injury-free, this is going to be a great year."

It was heading that way, too. Beebe played in twelve games and started in four, including the game against the New York Giants on December 17, when he caught a forty-three-yard touchdown pass from Frank Reich in the second half to secure the 17-13 upset win.

Staring up at the rambunctious crowd from the end zone, Don was awed, excited. His eyes rose higher, and suddenly a wave of gratitude washed over him. He fell to one knee. He bowed his head and closed his eyes, tuning out all that was around him.

"Lord, thank you for giving me this opportunity to play football," he prayed. "Please let me glorify you … and not me."

Don was well aware of how fortunate he was and tried hard to keep it all in focus. Then, two days before Christmas, with a couple dozen of his family and friends in New York to celebrate the holidays, that lucky streak snapped, along with Beebe's left leg.

* * *

Don awoke the morning of December 23, 1990, wondering if he was living a dream he somehow didn't deserve – all because of that darn nightmare. Normally his sleep was solid the night before a game, although at times it would take him a good hour to drift off. But he rarely awoke in the middle of the night, and he certainly didn't have dreams that interrupted his slumber, especially ones that drove him to pacing the bedroom to break the rhythm of his racing mind.

This dream didn't make much sense. He was standing at the bottom of a hill — a steep sandy incline that seemed to go straight into a thick dark cloud. He called out for help. Suddenly, dozens of footballs started coming at him. Maybe hundreds. Zipping over his head. Landing with a thud at his feet. Sailing to his right and left. And try as he could to catch them, he came up empty handed as thousands of spectators — he could see none of their faces —yelled at him from the stands to pick it up, pick it up, PICK IT UP!

Don remembered another time he heard a voice telling him to pick it up – as his phone was ringing in the dorm room when he was packed and ready to leave his football dreams behind. But what did this command mean? Pick up what? Pick up the pace? Pick up the balls? Couldn't they see he was trying his best? But was his best good enough?

Don awoke, angry at himself for allowing self-doubt to interfere with needed rest. The clock read 5:23 a.m. He didn't even try to fall back asleep.

"Heavenly Father, if you've got another mountain for me to climb, I'm ready," he whispered so as not to awaken Diana. "Just don't make it too steep, please."

Don didn't tell his wife about the dream. And with so many guests staying at the house for the holidays, he quickly forgot about it. Diana, his mother and sisters spent most of the morning baking sugar cookies for the Christmas Eve celebration the following night. And his dad and brothers were piling red and green presents under the six-foot tree decorated from top to bottom with an assortment of colorful blinking lights newly purchased at Wal-Mart.

But he remembered the dream again as he walked onto the field at Rich Stadium a few hours later to greet the eighty thousand fans who braved the bitter cloudy day to watch their Bills take on the Miami Dolphins. One thing about Rich Stadium: it was notoriously unwelcoming for the visitors who stepped onto its turf. The blustery weather and rapid crowd gave the Bills a home field advantage like no other venue in the NFL, and Don was feeling that intensity like no other game. Maybe it was the nightmare that spurred him on. Maybe it was having so many of his family in the stands. Whatever the reason, he was having his best game of the year: three catches for seventy-four yards, and that was just the first fifteen minutes of the game.

Then, in the second quarter, the Bills ran a sweep to Beebe's side. His assignment was to block defensive back Tim McKyer, but Thurman Thomas cut underneath Beebe's block. Miami All-Pro linebacker John Offerdahl, scraping along the line of scrimmage, turned sideways in a lateral pursuit to cut Thurman off. He dove at the running back and missed. But Offerdahl got Beebe — all of Beebe, with most of the impact hitting Don around the knees.

Trainers, teammates, opponents — everyone heard the pop. But only Beebe felt his left leg split in half.

The pain hit instantly, swelling like a tsunami, washing over his body and drowning out all sound as it tried like the devil to pull him into darkness.

Beebe screamed. He begged God for unconsciousness that did not come. Grimacing, Don pulled his left leg up and watched as part of it flopped to the turf. He looked up and saw his quarterback kneeling over him. Frank Reich placed his throwing hand on Don's right arm, touching his head with the other. "I know this hurts," he said calmly. "But give it up to the Lord, Beebs. Give it up to the Lord right now."

In front of the stadium-packed fans, many still holding their breaths from the violent collision they had just witnessed, Reich began to pray. "Jesus, we remember the suffering you went through for all mankind. Please take away the pain Don is feeling now." He began reciting the Lord's prayer. "Our Father, who art in heaven …"

"Hallowed be thy name …" Beebe's whispers were tortured but he followed Frank's lead. Almost immediately, the pain began to retreat.

Don rolled over on his side and another gasp went up from the crowd as his injured leg bounced off the turf. Frank backed away as the first responders rushed the field. The pair of grim-faced paramedics lifted Don up and cautiously positioned him on the cart.

As Beebe was driven from the stadium, the fans, now applauding in support, were astonished to see him suddenly sit up. Smiling, he raised his right hand, fist clenched, and waved at the crowd. "Bee-BE. Bee-BE. Bee-BE," they cheered. The roar was thunderous, too loud for even the paramedics or trainers to hear the promise Don made to the fans, and to himself, before he entered the stadium tunnel. "I'm not done playing football," he said. "I will be back."

Once he was off the field, the pain returned with a vengeance, and it didn't subside at Buffalo General Hospital. The X-ray determined Beebe had broken both the tibia and fibula in his left leg. "I suggest you bite on a towel," the doctor told his patient as he pulled out an eight-inch needle. "This could possibly could be the worst thing you will ever feel."

The shot felt like a branding iron. Don clamped down on the cloth, tears pushing against his tightly-closed eyes. "We need to do surgery, Don, to set the broken bones," the doctor told him a few minutes later. "It would be best if we did that immediately."

Don felt defeated. But whatever was in that King Kong needle had taken the edge off the pain, and he was convinced he could postpone the surgery for a day or two. "Please, Doc," he begged. "I want to be with my family on Christmas."

It was against his better judgment, but the doctor, hearing Beebe's tone, was convinced arguing with this patient would be counter-productive. He ordered a cast for Beebe's left leg and sent him home.

Don spent the next twenty-four hours lying on the couch, surrounded by Diana, his parents and all his siblings. He tried to navigate the pain, but it was too much. His foot turned an angry blue. At midnight he called the hospital. Within a half-hour an intern arrived to remove the cast. The discoloration subsided but the pain persisted. At three in the morning, Diana convinced Don to call for help again. "I can't take it anymore," he told his doctor. "Please send over an ambulance."

Surgery was performed on Christmas morning at Buffalo General. A hospital was hardly the place anyone would want to spend the holiday, but at that moment, the greatest gift Don received was relief from the brutal pressure. The following day, as he lay in his hospital bed, another worry began to gnaw at him. The Bills had a shot at the playoffs. Maybe even the Super Bowl. He wanted to be there to help them reach that goal. It was something he'd dreamed about from the time he was a little kid. Now this: a hospital bed and, no matter how much he didn't want to think about it, a very uncertain future.

Still groggy from the anesthesia, Don could remember his dream from the night before. From the time he was a kid, Don's mom had made him aware of all those hurdles that get thrown into well-designed paths. God obviously had a plan. But why another mountain so soon after scaling the first one? Couldn't he have let Don enjoy a little more time on the top?

He heard a knock at his door.

"Don, are you up for a visitor?" asked Lydia, the petite dark-haired nurse on duty. "I've got one of your biggest fans here and she'd love to say hi."

Don spotted the wheelchair first. It was small. But it still overwhelmed the child sitting in it. "Don, this is Melissa Stanton, one of the bravest young ladies you'll ever meet," Lydia said. "Melissa, this is Don Beebe, one of the fastest football players we've ever had in Buffalo."

Beebe was drawn to the smile on the little girl's face … that and the metal brace that made a protective halo around her neck.

Melissa stuck out her arm and Don took her bird-like hand in his. He shook it gingerly for fear it would break. A victim of spinal cancer, Melissa was twelve but looked years younger. Her legs, as well as her arms, were thin as poles. But even the ravages of her disease couldn't detract from large, luminous brown eyes — or that beauty-pageant smile now covering her face.

"I'm sorry you broke your leg, Mr. Beebe," said Melissa, her expression of delight quickly morphing into concern. "The Bills could sure use you going into the playoffs." Like so many young cancer patients who have spent too much of their lives around adults in medical environments, she spoke with a maturity beyond her age. "But I'm awfully glad you are in this hospital today so I could meet you. Besides, I know everything's going to turn out OK and you'll be back playing football before too long."

Don glanced at his cast and thought about the fourteen-inch rod they had to insert in his leg. He thought about the sports announcers who over the previous thirty-six hours played his last game clip and solemnly announced the likelihood Don Beebe would never get his speed back after such a devastating injury. And without his speed, they surmised, Don Beebe was surely through in the NFL.

He looked into this little girl's eyes, twinkling with curiosity, with excitement for what life had to offer, even now, just days after yet another surgery to remove a cancerous growth on her spine. Don mentally opened the door in his heart, then shoved Old Man Pity out so he could make room for this new friend.

"I'm glad I'm here, too, Melissa," he said. "Because I think the both of us know a thing or two about comebacks, don't you?"

CHAPTER 22 – Bouncing Back

Melissa and Don developed a special bond after that first meeting. Twice a day, while he was in the hospital, she asked the nurses to wheel her into room 402 so they could chat about football or about the latest Baby-sitters Club book she'd read or about her dreams to someday see the Eiffel Tower.

Melissa wasn't afraid to talk about the cancer, either. "I've had eight surgeries so far," she said. "I'm not supposed to hear these things, but I know my heart stopped a couple times when I was being operated on. That's kind of weird, isn't it? To have your heart just stop. But then it started up again."

"And I'm glad it did," Don replied. "God knows an angel when he sees one. But he obviously has a plan for you here on Earth and he wants you to hang around with the rest of us mere mortals to teach us a thing or two."

Melissa didn't seem to hear his words. Her thoughts had gone somewhere else. "I just wish my mom didn't have to cry so much," she finally said. "Sometimes she doesn't know I am listening. She cries real quiet. But I can still hear her. That's why I try so hard. I don't want to see her sad."

The little girl amazed Don. Her courage, her maturity, her ability to discern what was important in life blew him away. But mostly, he was impressed by her compassion for others. She was concerned about him. Concerned about her mother and other family members. She talked about other children struggling with cancer she'd met on her many hospital adventures. "I like to cheer them up," she said. "If I can make them laugh or even smile, it makes me really happy, too."

Don thought about the road that stretched ahead for Melissa. Talk about a lot of tall mountains looming in front of her. He felt guilty when comparing them to his own situation. There were no more surgeries awaiting him. He'd already been to prom. He had graduated from high school and had fallen in love. Got married, went to college. All major milestones in life. This child may never experience any of them. Yet she always seemed to find ways to comfort him.

"Your injury is bad," she told him in her best doctor-to-patient voice. "But I watched you play and you're tough. I really know you're going to be OK."

"Melissa, you are a very brave girl," he told her on their last visit, the night before his release. "I think God did me a very big favor by bringing you into my life. Thank you for being my new buddy."

"Oh, thank YOU," she said. "I'm really glad we are going to be friends because now I can say I met someone who played in the Super Bowl. And the Bills are definitely on their way to the Super Bowl!"

It turned out, Melissa was spot-on. Despite the absence of Beebe's speed, Buffalo marched through the post-season schedule. And the entire city caught a severe case of playoff fever as their beloved Bills prepared to take on the New York Giants in the championship game on January 27, 1991, in Tampa Bay.

Melissa never got to see Super Bowl XXV in person, despite Don's attempts to get her and her family tickets. She was back in the hospital, undergoing yet another round of chemo. Don hoped she could watch the game on TV, because it was a great one, the lead bouncing back and forth like a ball in a Ping-Pong game. In the last two minutes, the Giants got into the end zone on a thirty-one-yard run to take a 20-19 lead. In a drive that started on the Buffalo ten-yard line, Jim Kelly marched his

Bills down the field to the thirty. With three seconds remaining, place-kicker Scott Norwood lined up a forty-seven yard field goal for the win ... only he was one lousy yard too far to the right. And the Bills walked away with what would be the first in a string of Super Bowl losses.

For Beebe, the defeat was particularly painful because he was forced to watch from the sidelines. Could he have made a difference in this game? The question would always haunt him, especially as he struggled to complete his rehabilitation.

The cast remained on for two months, but the rod would stay with him the rest of his life. By early spring, doctors told him the leg was healed enough for him to begin strength training. He had to make his leg stronger than ever. As with everything he did, Beebe attacked this new goal with a relentless fervor. For two hours every day he hit the weight room. Then, another two hours he'd run; alternating with hops that would put his full body weight on the vulnerable leg.

Punishing. Pounding, like a ruthless drill sergeant. Hour after hour. Day after day. He thought about Coach Craddock at Western Illinois University. "Hit it! Hit IT! Drive through it. How bad do you want it? Show me! "

Don grew weary of his leg screaming at him to stop. One night he dreamed again of the mountain. Only this time it was taller, darker. Don awoke and stuck in the tape of the commentators forecasting his NFL demise. He wondered what Melissa was doing right now. Sleeping like a baby, he hoped. "My hurdles are nothing compared to that little girl's," he would tell Diana when she'd beg her husband, his face contorted, to ease up, at least for a day. The mountains, he reluctantly learned, were all around him.

Then Don found a real steep hill, covered mostly in sand, within a quarter-mile of his parent's home in Sugar Grove. It was a tough climb —

so tough, his brother Dave couldn't make it all the way to the top, even on two good legs. But three times a week, most often in the morning, sometimes closer to dusk, Don challenged that forty-five-degree incline. The first few attempts, he didn't make it halfway up. But gradually the ordeal became more tolerable. After a few days of reaching the top on both legs, he tried scaling the hill on his left one.

One hop. Two hops. Three hops. Four. Five …. twenty-four. Twenty-five … .

Now he really did feel like a Pogo Stick. But he forced himself through this agonizing workout day after day — until the pain was reduced to a dull throb. Then he tried hopping down the hill, a trickier balancing act that applied even more pressure to the mending bone.

The assault continued until sweat poured from his face, blinding him. He rested and felt guilty for doing so. Often, he shut his eyes, daring his weak leg to give out. Sometimes it would. And the tumble would bring momentary relief.

But not all the time. One cold rainy evening, as darkness claimed what was left of the already somber day, Don, making his tenth trip down the hill, lost his footing on the wet terrain. He slid five yards. When his head hit the ground, a bolt of light exploded inside his brain. He lay motionless, his body on a sharp incline as rain washed over his face and mud slid into his sneakers.

He wondered if he had re-injured the leg. He wondered if he could even get up. Would his family know where to find him? He thought about the letter he'd received from Melissa the day before. She told him she was proud of his progress. "Keep up the good work," she wrote in her careful cursive. "I'm keeping you in my prayers every single night."

Don reached for his left leg and felt familiar movement. Slowly he raised his head, then his shoulders. He sat up. He looked back at the hill, its pinnacle obscured by the black sky. He rose to his feet, tested his bum leg. He began to hop — slower this time so he wouldn't slip again.

Barb, watching from the house, saw more than just an athlete in rehab. She saw her child in pain. She recalled those days of long ago, when she and his dad would watch Donny with the football in the back yard running plays well past dusk, demanding perfection, if not from his buddies, then certainly from himself. Some things never change, she sighed as she watched the lonely figure on the sand hill.

The rain began to fall harder.

"Honey," she called out to her husband who was watching TV in the living room. "Do you think you should go out there and tell Donny to come in? I'm afraid he's going to get hurt even more out there. I don't understand why that kid has to push himself so hard. Doesn't he realize he can always go back out tomorrow?"

Don Sr. looked up from the TV, eyeglasses perched on the tip of his nose. "You can never finish up today's work tomorrow, dear, because that would make it tomorrow's work," he said softy. "Don needs to do this. He'll be OK."

* * *

When Beebe reported for camp in July 1991, he was more than OK. He was on fire. He had dropped a couple of catchable passes his rookie year in big games and he couldn't forget that feeling of failure. So even as he worked at forcing strength back into his legs, he also concentrated on his hands. The goal was to make them tough enough to catch any bullet thrown his way, yet supple enough to control the short, quick passes that too often get dropped.

Every day he'd fire up the JUGS machine. And Diana, his father, brothers, even his mother would take their turns running the apparatus that spit out ball after ball after ball in rapid-fire succession. He'd catch one hundred at a time. If he muffed even one, he'd order them to set up the machine again. Then he'd catch another one hundred. At the end of a long week of repeated drills, he could stand right next to the machine and snag the footballs — using one hand only — as they were spit out at sixty miles per hour.

"It's all a mental thing," he'd tell his sister Beth, recalling the words of his favorite soke. "If you say you can't, then chances are, you won't. I've got to be able to know in my mind that I can catch anything thrown my way."

The student had learned his lessons well. On September 8, in the second game of the NFL season, against Pittsburgh, Beebe caught ten passes for one hundred and ten yards, tying a Bills record with four touchdown receptions. And Kelly, who ended the night with an equally incredible six touchdown passes, slapped Beebe so many times on the back in the locker room afterward, Don started to feel like a well-worn punching bag. But it was all worth it. That night, while watching ESPN's "NFL Primetime," Don couldn't help but grin as Chris Berman, running a tape of Beebe being carted off the field at the Miami game almost nine months earlier, humorously chastised his viewing audience for their pessimism.

"All you people who doubted Don Beebe, who thought his career was over? NOT!"

CHAPTER 23 – Speaking of Heart

It was no surprise Don Beebe and Frank Reich would become roommates and best friends. The relationship began in that 1989 mini-camp just a few weeks after Don signed with the Bills. After practices, the two men were among a small group who played golf to unwind from the stress of the day.

The Bills' organization, unlike many other NFL franchises, didn't care if the players left the complex to go off and have a little fun. The athletes needed a chance to relax and get football out of their minds, Levy insisted. And this team, perhaps more than the majority of their NFL colleagues, could handle that extra freedom. That's because most had their heads on straight when the helmets came off, a fact the coach would later say helped them gel as a team and lead to a four-year run as AFC champs.

Both the rookie and the four-year-veteran were quiet men with strong family values who possessed equally solid work ethics. They knew how to tell a joke and take one. Neither drank or smoked. They weren't flashy or loud. And they didn't seek out the attention that seemed to follow so many who collected a robust paycheck by donning an NFL uniform on Sunday afternoons.

What drew the five-foot-ten receiver and the six-four quarterback even closer, however, was their faith. Just weeks after Don arrived for summer camp, Frank asked him and Diana to join the couple's Bible study group that met once a week

It was here, while listening to others share their own stories that Beebe began another chapter in his faith journey. Playing in the NFL was not a normal nine-to-five job, by any means. It is a profession that showcases human strength but exposes their weakness. It is a profession rife with the Old Testament's Seven Deadly Sins, most notably, lust, greed, envy — and of course, pride.

The problem was, that last sin, while it may be a tool of the devil, is absolutely essential, for if a professional athlete enters the battlefield without a Herculean dose of self-confidence, he surely will be destroyed. So how do you maintain humbleness in a profession that is built on an all-consuming drive to be the best of the best? Throw in every money-hungry agent or overzealous fan in a tight sweater and you've got unfriendly terrain, especially for the Christian athlete.

It's not like Beebe was shocked by the behavior of the opposite sex once he joined this most elite of professional athletes. Even at tiny Kaneland High, surrounded by fields of the Midwest's golden corn, there were plenty of girls with less than wholesome ideas about the cute jocks who walked their hallways. And the older the females got — whether it was at Western, AU or Chadron State — the more aggressive some of them became when they sauntered within striking distance of a letterman's jacket.

But those groupies were like Pippi Longstocking compared to the females who gathered around NFL players. Beebe saw it at the Combine, but was only tangentially aware of the scores of women — many of them drop-dead gorgeous — who were drawn to beefy athletes like bees to honey. His focus was on far different things, as it was when he moved to Buffalo, where it became even more apparent that women of all ages, races and dress sizes were available any time of the night or day.

He would have been blind to miss it. Women threw themselves at the players wherever they went; airports, restaurants, private parties or press conferences. They were standing outside stadiums, hotels, coffee shops and grocery stores. And their phone numbers on perfume-scented notepaper or their lingerie would even get to places they couldn't crash.

Beebe never received any underwear in the mail, but he certainly got his share of photos, locks of hair and marriage proposals, via the U.S. Postal Service or FedEx. And he got plenty used to the giggly, big-haired fans who would bat their fake lashes while approaching for an autograph, then conveniently lean over for maximum exposure as they asked for a signature.

"You just learn to avert your eyes," he laughed when the Still brothers quizzed him about his new lifestyle on that first trip back home. "And I never sign anything I wouldn't want my wife to see me autographing."

Diana was also well aware of these aggressive females, but wives of NFL players have to find their own level of trust. For the Beebes, infidelity was never an issue they needed to discuss. "Why would I be tempted by any of these females when the best-looking woman God ever made is right by my side?" he proudly declared.

As his rookie season progressed, Don also realized that, as you build a reputation for being a strait-laced family man, those temptations become fewer and farther between. The same couldn't be said for some of his teammates, including a few married ones, who had a different woman waiting for them in the lobby of every hotel they stayed. This close-knit Buffalo team was, for the most part, a wholesome group, at least when compared to some of the other franchises. Still, the bad behavior, including late-night partying with drugs and alcohol, was prevalent.

It bothered Don, but what these teammates did in their own time was not his business. "It's tough to watch sometimes," he told Diana, just weeks after the season began. "But if I become judge and jury over what some of these guys are doing, what kind of a Christian does that make me?"

Don quickly earned a reputation as a guy who could hang with anyone. He didn't drink booze, but the party boys loved him. He was a conservative white guy from suburbia whose ready smile and quick wit made him a favorite with just about everyone on the team – whether they were black players raised on urban streets or Irish Catholics from the hills of Pennsylvania.

Still, because of the many ethical landmines that awaited NFL players, Beebe felt a need to bond with other Christian athletes. And because of the worldwide adulation that is heaped upon the players, these men of faith are acutely aware their celebrity status provides them with a unique chance to bring their message of salvation to others. When Bills Chaplain Fred Raines realized the depth of Don's spiritual commitment, he and Frank recruited their new teammate to join the organization's Christian speaking circuit, where he could share his unique personal story as well as his faith journey with others.

But the NFL rookie was no more comfortable standing in front of a group of strangers than he was as a kid in high school — no matter how much he believed in the message. The night before he and Frank drove to Warsaw, New York, to speak to a group at the First Baptist Church there, Beebe spent the time between dinner and bedtime trying to figure out a way to get out of the engagement.

He knew that a downright lie was out of the question. Even going with a small fib would be tough to reconcile. So he could only hope that all-too-familiar churning in his stomach was signaling the onset of a contagious disease. If that was indeed the case, then surely he couldn't take the risk of spreading this horrendous virus to an innocent audience, could he?

Diana didn't buy any of it. "Talk to Frank. Pray about it," she told her husband. "I know you dread public speaking, but you have so much to share with others."

On the ninety-minute ride to Warsaw, Frank gave a similar pep talk to his friend. "The problem, Beebs, is you are making this about yourself. It's about your fears. You've got to give it up to the Lord. Once you understand that, it gets a whole lot easier."

When the two men arrived at the large stone church, built more than one hundred years earlier, they were greeted by a warm welcome from the standing-room-only crowd of two hundred-plus who had gathered in the newly remodeled basement. Reich took the microphone first and spoke fervently about his faith journey with the same confidence and poise he demonstrated on the playing field.

His message was one he and Don often talked about. "Unfortunately, too many of us aren't listening when the Lord is trying to talk to us," he told the group, "because we have so much chatter from the outside world drowning him out."

Frank, used to speaking in large groups, could not only move his audience emotionally, he engaged the crowd in a comfortable interchange that drew a round of hearty applause when he finished. Don, in the meantime, grew increasingly aware of his own shortcomings — and the uncomfortable urge to hit the men's restroom.

There was no time for such options. As Frank began introducing him, Beebe — face flushed, hands clammy — was all but convinced that even if his bowels cooperated, he'd start hyperventilating at any moment. Or just as bad, he'd be incapable of uttering a single syllable after taking the microphone. Instead, when he opened his mouth, the words flowed as if they were displayed on an ESPN teleprompter.

"Psalms 46:10 tells us to be still and know that God will speak to us," he began. "When I was hanging siding for my brother-in-law, I knew I had to go back to school and start playing football again. I wasn't sure how I was supposed to do that, though. I was unfocused, confused and off track in so many aspects of my life. I started talking to God, asking the Lord to open up some doors and show me what to do. Then, a week later, I got a call from Western Illinois, saying they wanted me to come back to school there. I was ready for college again at that time. I prayed hard, and I became comfortable with my decision. And when that happens, the Spirit is letting you know what the Lord wants you to do."

As he picked up momentum, Beebe became aware of the impact his words had on the audience. A burly man with a thick, red beard and ruddy complexion nodded his head when Don challenged his listeners to give up everyday struggles to the Lord. A woman clutching a tissue dabbed at her eyes. A young man leaning against the back wall, his face peppered with acne, bowed his head when Don spoke about living a spirit-filled life, despite the mistakes we all make.

"In all ways acknowledge him," Don fervently advised, "and he will set your path straight."

As Beebe concluded his thirty-minute talk, the crowd came to its feet. Over on the side, Frank smiled as if to say, "See. What did I tell you?" And for the first time, Don realized the power of his testimony.

"This is what it's about, Frank. I realize that," said Don, barely able to contain his excitement on the midnight ride home. "My story means something to others, and if I can use my platform as an NFL player to reach people, then I need to do this more often."

Reich nodded but threw a word of caution to his friend. "Your most difficult struggle," he warned, "is remembering that none of this is about you. It's not about the hype or the fans in the stands. It's not about your stats or your name in the paper the next day. It's not even about that standing ovation you received in there. It's easy to get confused. It's easy for us to want to do things the way we think they should be done. But God is in control. And when you turn it all over to him, all the rest of it makes perfect sense."

Don found a sense of comfort that evening. No matter what his future in the NFL held, no matter how the path to this point had veered and grown rocky, he knew this was exactly where he needed to be.

"It's all starting to make sense," he told Dan when he spoke to his brother early the next morning. "I'm living a long way from Sugar Grove, but all of a sudden, I feel like I'm finally home."

CHAPTER 24 – Searching for Momentum

Diana tried not to show it, but she was worried. Don's leg injury that had sidelined him for most of the 1990 season did not bother her so much as all the head injuries he sustained over his years in the NFL. Six major concussions. So many smaller ones, it was too hard to count.

Don was small but scrappy — and that can be an unhealthy combination on a professional football field. Even Kelly, one of Beebe's biggest fans, worried about Don's vulnerability on the field. "Don't be going and doing something stupid out there today," he lectured his speedy wide receiver before each game. "Pull that hamstring again and you won't be doing a thing to help this team – or my stats for the season."

Still, despite the myriad injuries that some would say eventually denied him Pro-Bowl status, Beebe always bounced back, helping to sustain the Bills' four consecutive playoff runs.

In 1991, with four games left and a good shot at breaking fifty receptions if the Bills made the playoffs, Beebe snapped his collarbone in a 41-27 win over Miami. Rehabbing with the same determination he'd displayed earlier, he was back in uniform in time for the playoffs, and went on to lead the team in postseason receptions. And this time, he and his teammates were determined to come away with a victory when they made it back to the Super Bowl in January 1992.

It turned out to be one of the most embarrassing days of Don's career — and he blamed only himself for getting caught up in the hype that was the hallmark of this sport. Instead of concentrating on game preparations, Don's focus was overseeing the itineraries of the dozens of family and friends arriving in Minneapolis to watch the Bills take on the

Washington Redskins in Super Bowl XXVI. Even hours before the game, Beebe was busy fielding phone calls from out-of- town guests with last-minute requests or concerns. Add that to the orgy created by television cameras and swarms of eager reporters and photographers from around the world, Don was no more ready for this game than he had been a year ago when he was standing along the sidelines with his bum leg.

His teammates were not prepared, either. Although Beebe registered his first Super Bowl touchdown, with a short spiral from Kelly in the fourth quarter, the play meant little to Don. Thanks to six turnovers, the Bills took a thrashing, with the final score 37-24. And the press — yes, even the players themselves — were beginning to wonder if this team had what it took to be champions.

The 1992 season was another roller-coaster ride. Still plagued by injuries, Don missed three games with a hamstring pull, but tallied four one-hundred-yard games, as Buffalo ran up an 11-5 record in the regular season. But the Bills didn't have momentum going into the playoffs. They lost three of their last five games in 1992, the season-ender being a 27-3 shellacking by the Houston Oilers on December 27 at the Astrodome.

And, as luck would have it, in the wild card game that decided who would make it to the playoffs, the embattled Bills went head to head again with the team that had just given them a sound thrashing.

To many Buffalo fans, including the players, themselves, it would take more than a few prayers to pull this one off. What was called for was a bona fide miracle.

CHAPTER 25 – Coming Back Big

As much as he hated to admit it, Don was starting to get annoyed with Frank Reich. For almost a week, his friend had been humming some Michael English song he'd heard on the radio and complaining about the fact he couldn't get the words or melody to "In Christ Alone" out of his mind.

In Christ alone will I glory;
Though I could pride myself
In battles won.
For I've been blessed beyond measure;
And by His strength alone, I overcome.

If he'd heard Frank singing it once, he had heard it a hundred times. Only, there were words and phrases missing and that's what was driving his roommate absolutely bonkers.

"So try replacing it with 'When the Saints go Marching in,'" joked Beebe. "Or how about a little Mariah Carey love song."

It's not like the two men didn't have other things to think about. Especially Frank. The Bills, after an up and down season, had a chance to get back to the Super Bowl for the third year in a row. But first they had to get past the Houston Oilers on Sunday in a wild-card game that would determine who would advance in the playoffs. And with Kelly out because of a strained knee, it fell to Reich to get the job done.

"Frank, forget it, already!" he told his friend as the week wore on and the quarterback continued to obsess about the missing words to the

150

song. "This is the biggest game of your life and you need to be thinking about other things besides a few mysterious lyrics."

The advice was solid, but totally ignored. The night before the game, Beebe slept fitfully himself as he listened to Frank toss and turn in the room they shared at the Buffalo Sheraton. On the morning of the game, Beebe awoke before the alarm went off and stared at the clock in the dark hotel room. Not quite 6:30. He thought about pulling the blankets up extra tight and grabbing another forty-five minutes of shuteye before having to even think about going down to the team breakfast. He looked over at the other bed, surprised to see nothing but rumpled covers and both pillows on the floor.

Beebe crawled out of bed and checked the bathroom. No Frank. He noticed the security lock on the hotel door was flipped. He opened the door and looked up and down the hallway. Still no Frank.

Puzzled, he returned to his room and noticed Frank's coat was missing. It's too early for breakfast and way too early to head to the stadium, he thought. Don threw on his brown parka, grabbed his gloves and headed downstairs. No Frank in the lobby.

"What the heck," Don mumbled, now beginning to worry. It was January 3, 1993, and a biting wind hit him in the face as he exited the hotel's revolving doors. The snow that had started to fall in the middle of the night was swirling like cotton candy, creating waves of white mounds that transformed the parking lot into a mosaic. It was cold. Freezer-burn cold. He blew air out his mouth and watched it form a cloud. He scanned the parking lot and spotted Frank's Cherokee sitting in the same spot he'd parked in the night before, with gray smoke blowing out the exhaust pipe.

"What the heck," Don repeated, his curiosity mounting.

He walked over to the car, and as he drew closer, he noticed the windows were defrosting enough to see the figure of a man in the driver's seat. He could also hear the faint sound of music coming from the interior.

"WHAT THE HECK," he muttered yet a third time. Don gently tapped on the driver's window. "Frank," he called out, his words muffled by the strong wind. "Frank, open the door. What in blue blazes are you doing in there, man?"

The window glass slowly slid down to reveal Frank's somber face and Michael English's voice. *In Christ alone will I glory ... Though I could pride myself in battles won...*

"I couldn't get the song out of my mind," his friend said. "I had to know what the rest of the words were. It was driving me crazy. So I came out here and put in this CD."

"But it's stinking cold out here, bro," Don replied, blowing into his frigid hands that were starting to sting. "You need to come inside. We've got a big game today, in case you forgot."

Frank held up the playbook that had been on his lap. On one of the inside pages were words scribbled in pencil, too scratchy for Don to make out. "I can't explain it, but the Lord wants me to write these lyrics down," Reich said. "I don't know why, but I just know I have to get the words to this song."

"You wrote the words in the playbook?" Don asked, his confusion apparent.

Reich nodded. "I had to replay the song about ten times."

Don stared at his roommate, wondering for a moment if his friend was sleepwalking or had lost his mind. But all he said was, "So, did you get it all?"

"I think so. Geeze, what an incredible song it is. It's about all the things we talk about, Don. About putting all our trust in the Lord. About how none of this is important unless we are doing it in God's name. And it hit me like a ton of bricks, that I have to share these words with others. Only, I don't know how I'm supposed to do that."

"That's great," Beebe said. "But seriously, man, it's cold out here and I think God wants more than anything for you to get inside and get ready for the game."

As it turned out, Frank was more than ready.

The playoff battle between the Bills and Oilers began as miserably as the blustery weather. Like their previous meeting, Buffalo was getting thumped by their opponents. And at halftime, with the score 28-3, it looked like the season was quickly coming to an end.

"So where do you think we're going to be playing golf next week?" wide-out Steve Tasker joked with Beebe as they jogged into the locker room.

"All I know is Coach isn't going to have too many nice things to say in there," Don replied. "We're going to get our butts chewed and it's not gonna be pretty."

The mood in the locker room was as chilly as the frozen field. The fans didn't exactly give the team a warm greeting, either, when the players took to the field twenty minutes later to begin the second half.

Back out on the frozen turf, Frank provided little reason for anyone to cheer. On the fifth play of the third quarter, Houston's Bubba McDowell intercepted one of the quarterback's passes and ran it back for a touchdown, making the score 35-3. And the Buffalo crowd, toes and fingers numb with cold, began heading for the exits. Judging by the mumbling along the Bills sideline, the team didn't want to be there any more than the fans. All except for Frank, who tried to drum up enthusiasm with every icy breath he took.

"C'mon, guys. All we have to do is start making plays. Let's get some first downs. Score a few points. We're getting the snot kicked out of us — the least we can do is make it respectable."

And so they did. The Bills scored a quick touchdown after the wind turned Oiler place-kicker Al Del Greco's kickoff into a squib. The Bills recovered at midfield and scored on a ten-play drive, capped by Kenny Davis' one-yard plunge.

Then, on the ensuing kickoff, Bills' place-kicker Steve Christie tried an onside kick and recovered it himself. After three plays, Reich turned to Don in the huddle. "It might be coming your way, Beebs. Get ready."

The ball was supposed to go to tight end Pete Metzelaars, but he was too closely covered. Reich's eyes scanned the field. He saw that Beebe, pushed out wide, was open. He launched a high arc, and Don easily snatched the ball from the air, running it effortlessly into the end zone for a thirty-eight-yard touchdown.

Reich hit Andre Reed for two more touchdown passes — and suddenly those fickle fans who had jumped ship were now clamoring to get back on deck. Most of them were either in the parking lot or already on the road heading home when they realized — either from the roar of the crowd still inside or from their car radios — they were missing what would eventually become the largest comeback in a playoff game in NFL history. And they didn't take no for an answer when security tried to keep them from re-entering the stadium.

The frost-bitten fair-weather fans did whatever they could to get back in, including scaling the twelve-foot fences in Rambo-like fashion.

By the time regulation play had run out, the score was 38-38 and the eighty-thousand-seat stadium was nearly filled again.

Overtime began with a coin toss that gave the ball first to Houston. But Buffalo's defense held the Oilers. Then Reich, after masterminding the dramatic comeback that tied the game, led his team downfield again ... enough for Christie to nail a forty-three-yarder to win the game for the Bills.

Bedlam broke out at Rich Stadium, as fans flooded the field already occupied by the still-stunned players who were falling over each other in disbelief. The media jumped into overdrive as cameras popped and announcers stumbled over their words trying to come up with the right superlatives to convey what had just happened. Only one man seemed to take it all in stride.

Later, while walking slowly toward the media room, where he would be expected to answer the questions most likely to make the front pages of sports sections across the country, Frank Reich stopped when he saw Don. "Tell 'em I'll be there in a sec, Beebs, but I need to go back to the locker," he said. "I have to grab the song because now I know what I'm supposed to do with it."

Reich turned, and jogged back to the locker room, grabbed the piece of paper that contained the words to the hauntingly beautiful song he'd copied from his playbook. A few minutes later he faced the TV cameras.

"Before I start to answer any of your questions, I need to read something," he stated. Then he unfolded the crinkled paper and spoke to the nation.

In Christ alone will I glory;

Though I could pride myself in battles won.

For I've been blessed beyond measure;

And by His strength alone, I overcome.

Oh, I could stop and count successes;

Like diamonds in my hands.

But these trophies could not equal;

To the grace by which I stand.

In Christ alone I place my trust;

And find my glory in the power of the cross.

In every victory let it be said of me

My source of strength; My source of hope

Is Christ alone ...

After finishing the song, Frank slowly refolded the piece of paper and tucked it inside his coat pocket. Raising his eyes, he grinned at the sea of journalists. "Ok, fellas …Now what was it you wanted to talk about?"

Don (center) with brothers Dave, Dan; and sisters Diane, Beth

Don's parents, Barb and Don Sr.

Don's senior year at Kaneland High School - 1983

Running at Kaneland with farm fields in the background

Kaneland Parents Day –1983

Diana cheering at Kaneland High School

Don and Diana at a high school dance – 1983

Kaneland Coach Joe Thorgesen working with
Don on fundamentals

Western Illinois Coach Bruce Craddock

Don at a pre-draft workout with Bills Coach Nick Nichalau

Bill Giles – NFL Combine Scout – with Don

The Beebes celebrate on NFL Draft Day

Don and Diana interviewed for TV on Draft Day

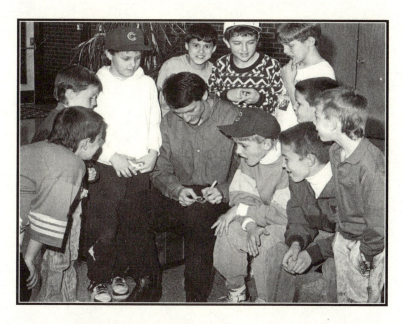

Don signing autographs for children at Chadron State

Chadron State Coach Brad Smith and Don with Chadron President
Sam Rankin in Buffalo

Don Beebe's first NFL catch is a 63-yard touchdown bomb

Don catches a record four touchdowns against the Pittsburg Steelers

Don's shoes from his record-setting "Mud Bowl" against the 49er's

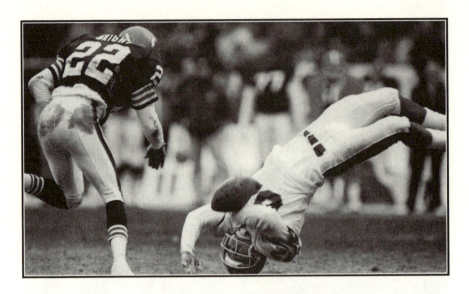

The iconic "Pogo Stick" play

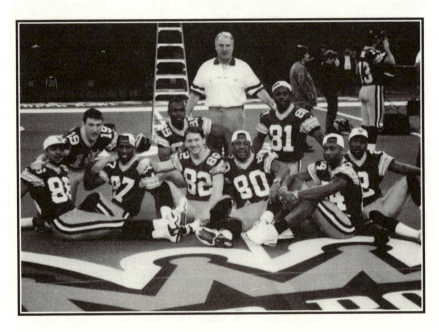

Super Bowl receivers – Green Bay

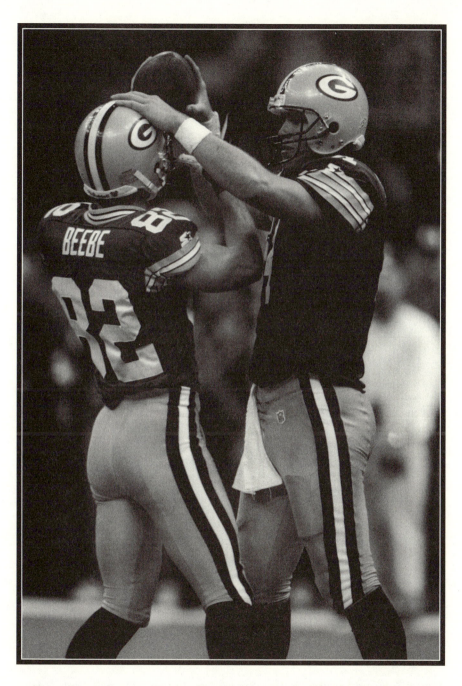

Brett Favre honors Don with the game ball after the last snap in
Super Bowl XXXI

Don holds the Lombardi Trophy on the plane on the ride home after
winning Super Bowl XXXI

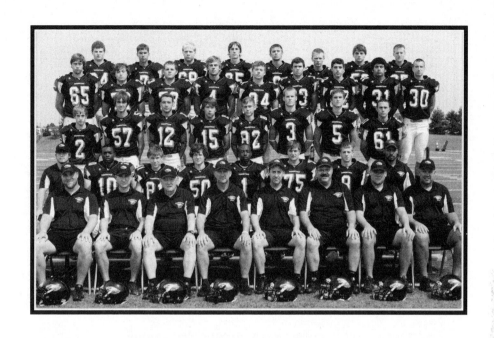

Coach Beebe with Aurora Christian's Illinois 3A 2011 Champions

Don and family on Graduation Day at Chadron State

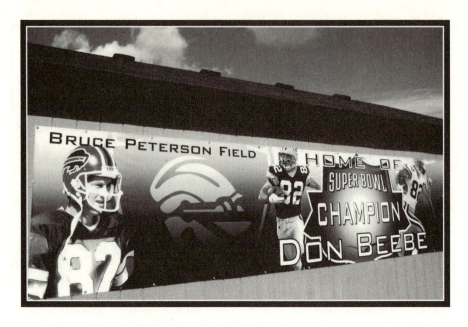

Kaneland High School football stadium dedication to Don – 2012

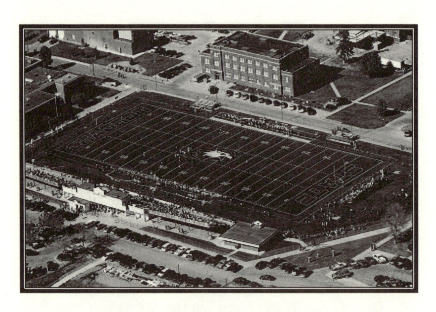

Don inducted into Chadron State's Hall Of Fame - 2000
Football stadium named in his honor

Don and former Super Bowl foe Leon Lett met after 20 years to film an upcoming documentary on their famed Super Bowl XXVII play. Over five days of filming, the two men realized how much they have in common, including a love for working with kids.

Leon driving Don on Super Bowl XXVII Reunion Publicity Tour

FRANKLIN GRAHAM CRUSADES - GREEN BAY & BUFFALO

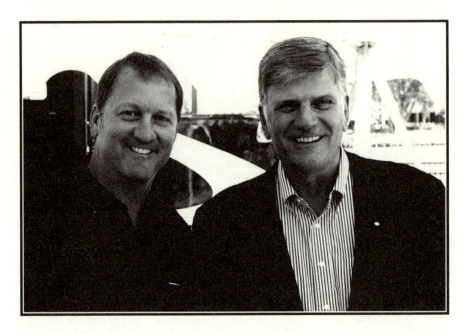

Don and Franklin Graham after Don spoke at Rock The Lakes Crusade

Tommy Coomes (Tommy Coomes Band) Ken Barun (Chief Of Staff)
Jim Gibson (Big Talk Publishing CEO) and Don

"Six Rings From Nowhere" Documentary Team
Jim Gibson; Dr. Chiann Gibson; Denise Crosby; Leon Lett; Don Beebe
Back row Trevor Matich; Leon Lett

A FRIEND NEVER FORGOTTEN

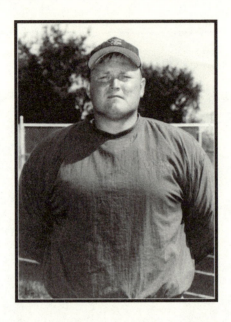

Don's best friend Jeff Still was killed
by a drunk driver not long after Don won the Super Bowl.
Below, Jeff is #78 at top left, cheering Don on

CHAPTER 26 – Fielding A Dream

After the game that Buffalo fans and other would simply refer to as "The Comeback," Don Beebe was more excited than he'd ever been in his football career.

The team was pumped up, as well. Buffalo went on to beat the Steelers 24-3 in Pittsburgh and the Dolphins 29-10 at Miami. That meant Beebe and the Bills were going to get yet one more shot at a championship trophy. And this time, it would be played on the field of a little boy's dreams: Rose Bowl Stadium in Pasadena.

Because Super Bowl XXVII was in Southern California, as opposed to frigid Minneapolis, there was no shortage of family and friends vying for tickets, including his high school football and basketball coaches, Joe Thorgesen and Bob Pederson. And Brad Smith, still coaching at Chadron State, wouldn't have missed it for the world. But Beebe was determined to not repeat last year's fiasco when his focus derailed. "Tell me who's coming," he told Diana. "But I don't want to know anything else. You handle all the details and just let me concentrate on the game."

That was a whole lot easier said than done. For an entire week, Diana took on the role of a CEO's assistant, arranging tickets on the phone, checking into hotels, car leases and even passing out maps to all the must-see places in sunny L.A. In addition to dealing with the all-consuming media-day blitz, Don felt like he was attending reunions every night at five-star resorts. One night he was playing eighteen holes at prestigious Riviera Golf Club with some teammates. The next night he was getting in a few holes with his brothers and good friend Mike Walker at a course that offered lights for late-night tee-times.

But when Beebe walked into the stadium hours before kickoff, all thoughts of birdies and bogeys evaporated as he took in the iconic stadium of the Rose Bowl. A smaller-than-average white guy from a no-name Nebraska college, he was well aware he didn't make it this far in his unique journey into the NFL without being a fierce competitor.

He was here for one reason: to help the Bills finally win a championship.

Don's thoughts were interrupted by whoops and hollers from a huddle of fans who had positioned themselves in the stands above the entrance to the locker rooms. Their excitement was directed at the Dallas players now popping out of the tunnel: Troy Aikman. Emmitt Smith. Michael Irvin. Known as "The Triplets," these future Hall-of-Famers sauntered onto the field as if they owned it. Following closely behind them was a hulk of a man with No. 78 on his T-shirt. Leon Lett. The Big Cat.

Don knew a few things about the Big Cat, and was surprised at how closely the Alabama athlete's life mirrored his own. Lett was also raised in a small town, Fair Hope. He too quit football to become a manual laborer, laying sod in 100-degree weather as a landscaper, before returning to the sport he'd loved since he was a small boy watching Terry Bradshaw and Roger Staubach work their magic for the Cowboys. Also like Beebe, Lett was drafted in the NFL out of a small Midwest college, Emporia State in Kansas, which lies between Wichita and Topeka.

Likewise, Lett was a fierce competitor.

As the Big Cat walked past Beebe. Don raised his eyes to meet the big man's gaze and nodded.

Lett glared. Don knew Lett would be menacing. Lett knew it, too. But neither had an inkling that, before the game was over, they would be forever locked together in the pages of NFL history.

CHAPTER 27 – Running on Faith

As he took a turn around the field before pre-game warm-ups, Don could feel that familiar surge of adrenalin. And it still flowed forty minutes later as the team gathered around Marv Levy while the Bills' head coach led his players in the same prayer that was recited at every game for the last six years.

"Our Father, who art in heaven," the baritone voices rumbled. "Hallowed be Thy name, Thy kingdom come "... Silence followed the final Amen. And it lasted long enough for the players to take in the crescendo of anticipation permeating the walls from the standing-room-only crowd now working themselves into a Super Bowl frenzy. In just a few minutes, he and the other Bills would run through the stadium tunnel — cameras rolling, hearts pounding — and be transformed into turf warriors. But at this moment, Beebe was only aware of his coach's words.

"Listen up, you guys. For three years we worked our butts off to get to this point ... and each time we got beat. We all remember how that feels. The fact we're even in this locker room today means this team is special. We lost two in a row. We're not losing three. We've earned it. Now let's go out there and take it!"

But all they ended up taking was yet another beating, this one among the most thorough and embarrassing in Super Bowl history, with a record nine turnovers, including four interceptions and five lost fumbles.

The Bills scored first early in the game, and even with the ridiculous number of turnovers, Dallas only led 14-10 with a little over three minutes left in the first half. But the Cowboys stormed downfield and scored in five plays. Then, Leon Lett forced a fumble at the eighteen-yard-line when he tackled Thurman Thomas. Aikman hit Michael Irvin for another touchdown to make it 28-10 at the half.

When the white-gloved Michael Jackson took the stage for the half-time show, Beebe wasn't the only one sitting in the locker dreading what was happening, yet again. Don's own game in the first half had been above average, at best. He had bumbled a tricky pass in the end zone during the second quarter; then made up those six points by snagging a forty-yarder on the last play of the third quarter. That put the Bills within striking distance at 31-17, and Beebe hoped this touchdown would spark a rally.

"We can do this! We can do this!" he yelled in the faces of the players as the deafening cheers from the Buffalo fans reflected their first glimmer of hope in two quarters. But after losing the big one too often now, the Bills seemed to have also lost their fire. It was a monumental flaw in this very good team that couldn't figure out how to be great.

It seemed as if every negative for the Bills resulted in a touchdown for the Cowboys. By the fourth quarter, after nine turnovers and with a score 52-17, Beebe felt only two things: embarrassment that so many people had come so far to see such a lopsided game; and frustration with his dejected teammates sitting along the sidelines with damp towels over lowered heads.

Halfway through the fourth quarter, the ship was sinking with no life boat in sight. It was the toughest of circumstances to play against. And as the clock ticked down, too many receivers showed little interest in catching the ball.

Don was not among them. With the Bills on the Dallas thirty-two-yard line, Beebe sprinted to the twenty after the ball was snapped. He was ready for the pass from Reich, but knew his friend was in trouble as soon as Frank's arm went back for the throw. Cowboys lineman Jim Jeffcoat hit him hard at the thirty-eight, and as the quarterback toppled to the ground, the ball landed at the feet of Leon Lett.

Don saw No. 78 scoop up the ball and head toward the Bills' end zone sixty-four yards away. He also saw there was no one in the big lineman's path. Beebe had no time to analyze his next move. He simply reacted.

"In life you often have only a split second to make decisions. Kids need to know just how important it is they make the right ones," Beebe would say later of his surprising pursuit of the big lineman. "Some of them can be life-changing."

Certainly that was the case for the small wide receiver. Don Beebe will be remembered forever for what happened in the next ten seconds. The play would go on to become one of ESPN's top moments in NFL history, played repeatedly on highlight reels year after year, long after bigger game-altering moments were forgotten.

Why it affected so many depends on who you ask. But for anyone who's ever cheered the underdog or read "The Little Engine that Could," this play was a high-profile reminder that even when situations seem hopeless, the real heroes are those who don't stop trying.

As Lett show-boated toward the end zone, Beebe knew he couldn't just let the big guy steal six points. Don was disappointed and discouraged. He was tired, too. But none of that had stopped him before. And it sure wasn't going to do so now.

Racing down the sidelines, the wide receiver caught up with Lett, who would later wonder "how I could possibly hear someone that small." And why, he would also ask, didn't Jimmie Jones even try to bump his pursuer out of bounds. Don knocked the ball from the Big Cat's grasp. It rolled out of bounds for a touchback, and even though none of this made a difference in the outcome of the game, the play impacted many lives.

It brought humiliation to Lett, as well as death threats from big-time gamblers who lost thousands of dollars because of a touchdown that would have earned Dallas the most points ever scored in a Super Bowl. Others made big money off the score's outcome. About a year after the game, Beebe returned to his locker to find a letter, along with a box containing a golf putter, both sent from a man who had made out big on Super Bowl XXVII.

"Was unemployed, didn't have much money, gambled the few thousand I did have. You won me a lot of money. In turn, I started making putters. In a year's time, my business has now flourished."

Beebe didn't care a lick about the gamblers, but he was delighted when he received letters from those who had used this Super Bowl play as a positive life lesson.

"My son and I never had a great relationship. Then I see this play where you don't give up. I show my son the play and say this is how you act in sports, and in life. Our relationship has changed because of it. You'll never understand how much your action meant to a lot of people."

"There was a reason I was put on that field at that time to perform that play," Beebe told his family. "I don't know why he chose me, but God was using this play as a lesson for all of us."

That unexpected Super Bowl moment would win Don Beebe the NFL's Unsung Hero Award. But for those who truly knew him, the play was not surprising at all.

"Don showed what a fighting spirit is all about," Coach Levy would say later when asked about the play. "He gave everything he had all the time."

CHAPTER 28 – Changing Direction

If there was one thing that was consistent in Beebe's NFL career, it was injuries. And he continued to be plagued by them through the 1993 season.

It started in training camp when he separated his shoulder; then he missed a couple more games with a pulled hamstring. But after returning to the lineup, he went on to catch thirty-one passes for 504 yards. And when the Bills rolled through the playoffs yet again, the team got another chance to face the defending World Champion Dallas Cowboys on January 30, 1994, in Super Bowl XXVIII.

This time, Beebe vowing more than ever to keep his concentration during the maniacal hype that surrounded the event, showed up to play. He tallied six catches for sixty yards and returned two kickoffs for sixty-three yards. But one strong performance was hardly enough.

The Bills led 10-6 at the half but fumbled the ball forty-five seconds into the third quarter. The Cowboys' James Washington picked it up and ran into the end zone. The Bills, as they seemed to do each year they faced adversity in the big game, deflated as quickly as a punctured tire. Emmitt Smith scored twice more and Eddie Murphy added a field goal for a 30-13 Dallas win, giving the Cowboys their second-straight Super Bowl victory over the Bills.

"We should have all been as focused as Don Beebe was," Jim Kelly told reporters after the game.

The wide receiver continued to work on that focus in the 1994 season. Beebe caught a career-high forty passes for a career-best 527 yards. In six seasons, he had racked up 983 career return yards and 2,537 receiving yards.

Injuries piled up, as well. Ten weeks into the 1994 season, he suffered yet another concussion in a game against the Jets and was forced to sit out the next three weeks. In his first game back, against the Dolphins, Beebe caught a seventy-two-yard touchdown pass from Kelly, and he finished strong, tallying eight catches for 111 yards in the season-ender against the Colts.

None of this was enough to keep the powers that be happy. Everyone from receivers coach Nick Nicolau to GM Bill Polian loved the die-hard wide receiver, and had nothing but praise for his character, both on and off the field. "You never turn down a chance to get a Don Beebe," Polian had told reporters and officials alike in the years since the 1989 draft. But after four Super Bowl defeats, followed by a season that ended without a playoff spot, it was obvious this team that had gelled so well and had won the hearts of many was heading for big changes.

Beebe was working out in the weight room on that overcast January day, 1995, when he got the call. "Don, if you're not too busy this afternoon, I'd like to chat for a few minutes," Levy said when Beebe answered his cell phone. "I'm in my office now, if you'd like to stop by."

The tone of the summons, friendly rather than curt, conveyed no hint of what the conversation would be about. Still, Don did not like the sound of this invitation. For one thing, he'd never even been inside the head coach's office in all his years playing for the man. And he had just finished up his second three-year contract with the Bills, which meant some sort of change was inevitable. Plus, his buddies Frank Reich and Pete Metzelaars had recently been released by Buffalo.

Don had reason for optimism. He knew that statistically, he'd come off his best season with the team. And because he had a solid relationship with Marv, he wasn't nervous when he walked into the big room at Rich Stadium that overlooked the field's parking lot.

Don greeted his coach and took a seat in the leather chair on the other side of Levy's large mahogany desk that was adorned with photos of his wife Fran and their children. "Nice office," he grinned, as he glanced at the gold light fixtures and wood-paneled walls lined with hundreds of books and framed photos touting Bills special moments.

Don was surprised at how calm he was; but then, no matter what his coach had to say, he knew the man was a class act who had a reputation for truly caring about the athletes he worked so closely with.

To the seasoned coach, this was the most distasteful part of his job. Even letting players go who lacked the character of a Don Beebe was hard. But it came with the territory. It happened to even the best of players and coaches, including himself. And he knew that how this young man bounced back would say more about him than any statistics he'd accumulated while playing for the Bills.

Levy got right to the point. "Don, you have to know how much I like you and respect you, not just as a player but as a man who has his priorities straight," said the coach, his hands now folded across his lap. "I've told you this before and I mean it completely. You are everything we want this organization to represent; and you have been an integral part of our success these past six years."

"Thank you, Coach," Don said, waiting for the blow he now figured was coming.

"I've got to tell you, it's always tough to let a player like you go. But as a staff, we've decided to go in a different direction. We are looking at signing some younger guys and want you to know that we'll do everything we can to make sure you end up with another great organization that deserves your character and talents."

Don knew his many injuries had not helped his chances of signing another contract, no matter how well he'd performed the previous year. There had been too many broken bones, too many concussions. And who's to say he wasn't one hard hit away from permanently retiring from this game he loved so much?

Still the news stung. Beebe had wanted to spend his entire career in Buffalo. It was a unique town that supported its sports teams like no other. And he had come to appreciate and enjoy genuine friendship with so many of the players and staff, from the equipment manager to the head trainer to the strength and conditioning coach. Now he would have to say good-bye to all of them.

They say the first phone call is the toughest. Diana, too, had made close friends here. Plus, she loved their two-story Tudor-style home on the quiet cul-de-sac on Pino Alto Court. This was where they lived when their first child Amanda was born five years ago; where they had brought baby brother Chad home just a year ago.

Diana would support him no matter where he went from here, even if that meant hanging up his spikes for good. And who knows, maybe she'd even be relieved. Although she didn't nag, she was concerned about the injuries, especially those to the head. "How many concussions can you take, until the damage is permanent?" she had asked after the hit knocked him out of play for a couple weeks. And now this low blow.

"Babe, they're not renewing my contract," he told his wife over the phone on the long ride back from the stadium.

"Oh, Don, no," she blurted, the disappointment clearly coming through the mobile phone. But the calm was back in her voice the next sentence. "We'll be fine, honey. Call Bob and let's figure out what we are going to do next."

186

That second call didn't bring quite as much apprehension. "We'll find a place for you," LaMonte told him when he heard the news. "You had some injuries, but if you look at your stats, they're pretty darn impressive."

Both agent and client decided their first choice was Green Bay. "They're not that far from getting to the Super Bowl," Don reminded LaMonte. "Plus, Green Bay is only three hours from Chicago, and it would be great to play close to home."

It didn't hurt that another of Bob's clients was Mike Holmgren, Green Bay's new head coach. Talks began almost immediately, but it became obvious early on the Packers weren't in the market for a new receiver; or at least, a five-ten white guy. It wasn't like a bunch of other teams were beating down the door to sign Beebe. He was fast, but he also came with a long list of injuries that made most organizations skittish about bringing him on board.

Don and Bob were thrilled when the call came from the Carolina Panthers, a newly-formed expansion team led by Polian that was opening its doors in Charlotte. The team had signed Pete in February and Frank the following month. When they flew Beebe down in April on a recruiting trip, it looked certain the three former Bills would be back together.

Plus, Diana and Don fell in love immediately with Charlotte and its friendly, down-to-earth residents. The offer, $1.3 million on a two-year-contract, made Beebe the team's No. 1 receiver. And he was pumped about being the go-to guy for the first time.

So there it was: A new start in a brand new stadium with three friends and former teammates playing together again. No wonder Frank Reich described it to the press as "a dream come true." Only, the stint in Carolina turned out to be more of a nightmare.

CHAPTER 29 – Changing Direction, Again

Don learned early in his rookie year the power a coach can have on an athlete's career. Not only could they play you or sit you, they also had the ability to make you look like a superstar on the field, or turn you into a toad.

In large part, it came down to their personal agendas, their biases or maybe just what side of the bed they happened to wake up on any given morning.

In Buffalo, Don had mostly benefited from coaches who appreciated his hustle and character. On more than one occasion he'd gone in for films on the Monday following a game and noticed that, even if he had not played the greatest four quarters on the field, his film didn't look all that bad. For a coach, it was easy enough to do: Stop the film and replay a good move, a decent catch or great pass pattern, and point out all the positives. Just as easily, they could quickly slide over that dropped pass, botched route or some other play where it was obvious the player was stinking up the joint.

It worked in reverse, too. An athlete may have had a good game, but by focusing on his one or two mistakes, the coach could give the impression this jamoke couldn't compete in a Pop Warner contest.

Don saw the red flags early on with the Panthers. While he had nothing but admiration for Polian and head Coach Dom Capers, offensive coordinator Joe Pendry and receivers coach Richard Williamson had a way of making him feel inferior from the get-go. In mini-camp that spring, he was taken aback by the coaching styles of the two men, who used intimidation and degradation to get their points across. Beebe felt like he had to prove himself on the field over and over again.

And things turned even worse when, in the first preseason game after training camp in August, he was injured, this time when he got drilled in the back while making a routine catch over the middle.

Funny, how he always heard the hurt before he felt it. CRACK!

NO! not again, he screamed silently, then waited for the pain he knew was coming. *Why, Lord, why me again?*

The broken rib took him out of action for three weeks. When he returned, his starting position had been taken over by Willie Green, a six-foot-four Mississippi recruit who had played for Detroit and Tampa Bay before landing with Carolina.

Don never got the job back again. No matter how hard he hustled at practice, no matter what kind of game he had, when he showed up in the film room, the coaches treated him like a rookie, highlighting his mistakes and fast forwarding through some outstanding catches.

Beebe didn't know why, either. Maybe it was his age. Maybe it was his size. Maybe they didn't like the color of his eyes. In the end it didn't really matter. It was humiliating — not to mention incredibly frustrating. But Beebe vowed to not let it get the better of him. As much as he wanted to get in the faces of these two coaches, he kept his cool and suffered in silence … almost in silence.

Except for Diana, who could sympathize as only a wife can, there was one other person who felt the same way. Frank had lost his starting position the third week to Kerry Collins, the Penn State standout drafted fifth overall in '95. And watching the way the coaches treated his friend was every bit as disheartening as his own experiences.

The situation only worsened as the season wore on. Beebe started in just one game, where he caught three passes, and played in only eight of sixteen games. It was a challenging year for the veteran receiver. When the season concluded, he had no choice but to begin thinking beyond the NFL.

First item on the to-do list: Get his degree. When Beebe was drafted in 1989, he promised both Diana and Coach Smith he'd head back to Chadron State to finish the twenty-one credit hours he needed to graduate. While playing for Buffalo, he never got the chance. The Bills were in the playoffs for all those seasons, except for last year, when Don had spent the post-season looking for another team.

Now with Carolina, he had no excuse. He packed up his young family and headed to Nebraska. He rented a two-bedroom ranch house just down the street from his former head coach and settled into life as a regular Chadron State student ... who happened to be an NFL player. Which is not exactly an everyday occurrence in this small prairie town. Everywhere he went, Don was treated like a celebrity, which any A-lister can tell you, has its pluses and minuses.

Classes alone kept him studying from morning to night. The schedule included market research, business law, micro economics and an English class. When he wasn't sitting in class or hunched over a small desk in his bedroom, Don was hitting the weight room or running. Student or not, he knew the older he got, the more competitive his chosen profession would become if he wanted to keep playing on Sundays. That was a question he'd begun to wrestle with in earnest. But it became more relevant when he got the call from his head coach.

Don was in the bedroom on the computer, writing a paper for his retail class, when it came in. Diana picked it up. "Don, it's for you," she yelled. "Coach Capers." A few pleasantries were exchanged. Then, as coaches are prone to do, Capers cut to the chase. "Don, we're going to release you."

The rest of the conversation was similar to the talk with Levy the previous season. He was a great athlete. He had great character. The team was going in a different direction, blah, blah, blah, blah. Only this time, the rejection felt different. The Bills chose not to renew his contract. In this case, the Panthers were outright cutting him. After saying good-bye to Capers, a man he truly appreciated for his professionalism, even in this uncomfortable moment, Don hung up the receiver and stared at the phone.

"What's going on?" Diana approached with caution, knowing the news was not cause for celebration.

"We got released today," he said, turning to his wife. "I guess I really shouldn't be surprised. But I've never been cut by a team in my life. This means they just don't think I'm good enough. And I gotta tell you, hon, that hurts a whole lot more than the last time."

His agent, as usual, didn't seem so devastated. "Thank God!" LaMonte yelled into the phone. "Listen Don, this was the best thing that could have happened to you. The Panthers were the wrong fit for you. I know it. You know it. For crying out loud, you were miserable there because they weren't using your experience or your speed. We're going to find a team that will — and the first one I'm talking to is Green Bay again."

The dialogue with the Packers went on for a couple of months. In the meantime, Beebe committed himself to the job that needed to be done at Chadron State. In addition to attaining a 4.0 GPA and earning a spot on the President's List, he found time to hold his first annual golf tournament that would eventually result in a brand new football stadium for the college.

On graduation day, thirty-year-old Don Beebe walked up to the podium, accepted his diploma and delivered the commencement speech at Chadron State. He was long past the days when he was petrified to deliver a message to an audience. And it was an especially exhilarating day because he'd just signed a contract with the Green Bay Packers.

Yet, as he packed up his young family for another move, Beebe had plenty of mixed emotions to accompany him on the trip back to the Midwest. He had not enjoyed his time playing football that one season in Charlotte. He had come to question many things in his life. Still, after hours of prayer and reflection, he realized his short stay with the Panthers had been a growing experience for him spiritually.

It was like a classroom laboratory, where he was forced to learn up close and personal what Frank and he would talk about in Buffalo. Their time in the NFL was not about accolades; nor was it about the stats or the positive press. He got none of that in Charlotte. The Lord, he now realized, wanted him to face a different kind of adversity — and to become a better man because of it.

"He's pointing to another path," Don had told Diana after the phone call from Capers. "I just hope Jesus gives me a hint of where the road is supposed to lead."

The night before the first practice of summer camp with the Packers, Beebe was still confused and despondent. He couldn't help but wonder if the passion that had driven him to succeed had somehow grown dim. And this was hardly the time for his light to fade. He knew he had to ride into Green Bay game-ready if he ever wanted a shot at playing. The team had enviable depth at his position. In addition to Pro-Bowler Robert Brooks, Antonio Freeman was proving his remarkable talents; plus the organization had just signed Desmond Howard.

Did he still have the desire to be a playmaker in the NFL? Beebe was thirty years old but he was also a husband and father to two little kids, with a third child on the way. And with camps taking him away for six weeks at a time, he was concerned about the lack of time he would be able to spend with his growing family.

Lying in bed, he decided that staring at the ceiling and calling out to God just wasn't going to cut it. He hopped out of the warm blankets, got down on his knees and prayed as fervently as he ever had. "Lord, if you want me to continue on in football, then give me the desire to go out and play it the way I need to — rejuvenated in spirit. You know me, Father, better than anyone. I can't play the game half-hearted."

He awoke the next morning with doubts still lingering. But when he reported for his first practice with the Packers at St. Norbert College less than ten hours later, Don was surprised by the wave of intensity he felt as he entered the stadium. It was a fire that had been missing the entire past season. Whatever Carolina had taken out of him was back, in full force. Don Beebe was ready to play some football in Green Bay.

But was Green Bay ready for Don Beebe?

CHAPTER 30 – Proving Value

When Beebe signed on with the Packers, he was convinced this storied football program, which had won more championships than any other in NFL history, was on the verge of another run at greatness. After winning the first Super Bowl against the Kansas City Chiefs back on January 15, 1967, the Green Bay juggernaut went on to repeat the feat with a Super Bowl II win against the Oakland Raiders. But after that, the Packers lost their mojo, becoming a losing team for much of the 1970s and 1980s.

All that changed, however, in 1992, when Mike Holmgren drove into town as head coach. And that same year, a young gunslinger by the name of Brett Favre signed on with the Packers after spending his rookie year in Atlanta. Then he took over as starting quarterback when Don Majkowski tore an ankle ligament in the third game of the season.

Beebe, added to the roster in 1996, was neither disappointed nor disappointing. Don earned respect and solidified a position on the team not long after he signed on with the Packers. Sports columnists for the Green Bay Press-Gazette questioned whether the small, aging, beat-up receiver could still run. No doubt there were some fans, not to mention a few coaches, asking the same questions.

Beebe supplied the answer at the first conditioning day, when the players all lined up for the shuttle runs and pro-agility testing to assess quickness and power. The latter required that each player sprint five yards to the right, touch a line, sprint back ten yards and touch the left hand to the ground, then dash back to the finish line.

Much like the NFL Combine in Indianapolis in 1989, Beebe had a lot to prove. And also like the Combine, he went into the event sure of himself and eager to show that he could play with the elite.

This time around, he was over thirty, with a history of concussions and broken bones. But this time around, he also had a pair of new Nikes on his feet instead of worn-out fishing shoes — and he had years of professional training.

He smoked the forty with a 4.25, the fastest time posted that day. Then, in case there were still those questioning his abilities, he broke the Packers pro-agility record with a 3.82. And for the first time since he'd entered the NFL, Beebe made it through his first training camp in August with no injuries. By the time the opening game of the season rolled around, Beebe had gone from the bubble guy, fifth or sixth on the chart, to the No. 3 receiver.

Packers fans are savvy, and they knew Beebe was a competitor. They'd seen him in the playoffs and four Super Bowls. And they held the Leon Lett moment in the highest regard. But Don recognized that if he was going to be part of this small-market team, he had to make a big impact. Right or wrong, good or bad, it was only natural: People were more likely to get excited about a shooting star than a fading one.

So early on in that 1996 season, Beebe said hello to the folks in Wisconsin by returning the opening kickoff ninety yards for a touchdown against the archrival Chicago Bears.

The next week in a game against San Francisco — on Monday Night Football — he was thrown into the starting lineup when Robert Brooks was injured on the first play. Beebe cruised into the end zone on a fifty-nine-yarder from Favre that gave him the right to throw his body into the stands in his first Lambeau Leap. And in typical Beebe fashion, he went on to have the biggest game of his career.

"Do you know how many yards you had?" an excited Lynn Swann, reporting for ABC Sports, asked him in a sideline interview immediately following this game the Packers won in overtime 23-20.

"I'm not sure," Beebe replied honestly. "Maybe 130?"

"How about eleven catches and 220 yards," Swann said. "You were like a man on a mission out there."

Coach Holmgren was equally enthused that he'd been able to pull off this upset on national TV without his star receiver. "That little guy can really play, can't he?" he grinned, as he looked at his newly-acquired player.

The newbie also had a few more talents the coach didn't know about; ones that would endear him to Green Bay fans in a totally different venue.

*　*　*

The marauders crept silently toward the house, lit only by the single porch light and the glow from the late-October moon.

It was Halloween night, 1996, and the monsters were only two of many freaks and spooks out on the streets of Green Bay in this early bewitching hour.

The shortest of the masked creatures was wearing an authentic-looking Packers jersey — with the name Favre scrawled across the back, followed by a big No. 4. His cohort — equally ugly — was also wearing a gold-and-green jersey; only, he had the name Beebe and No. 82 on the back. And surrounding them were a gaggle of children, as well as a wolfman, dressed in black corduroy and wielding a mighty sophisticated-looking camcorder.

The motley group approached the large Tudor and rang the doorbell. Coach Mike Holmgren appeared at the door, but he did not look happy to see his visitors. "You're not even going to believe this," he said. "We just gave out the last piece of candy. I'm so sorry, kids."

But the group of trick-or-treaters didn't take no for an answer. No matter how many times Holmgren said, "See you, guys," the masked figures didn't retreat.

"I'm sorry … bye, bye," the coach said again and again, this time the annoyance evident in his voice. "We don't have any candy left."

The football players didn't believe him. "What, no candy?" the smaller one whined. And the children chimed in: "Please, please, give us some candy!"

At one point, Player No. 4 started to step across the threshold of the door. "Look," the coach said sternly. "We don't have any left."

"What about Mr. Gills?" No. 4 asked innocently. "Does he have any candy?"

When Holmgren heard the trick-or-treaters use the name of his assistant coach, who was inside the house, he realized things were not as they seemed.

"Oh, geeze." He grinned, reached out and pulled the mask off No. 4 to reveal a laughing Don Beebe. Holmgren glanced over to the other now-revealed creature and stared into the face of his star quarterback.

The Halloween prank was just one of many shows taped by Channel 5, Green Bay's NBC affiliate that was home to the weekly "Don Beebe Show." The video aired a couple days after it was shot, with Favre sitting next to Beebe popping chocolate Reese's into his mouth when he thought the camera wasn't directed at him. It was a hit among the viewing Cheeseheads, just as most of Beebe's shows were that aired in Green Bay for about eighteen months.

NBC had approached Don about doing the talk show after executives learned he'd been successful with a similar stint in Buffalo for two years. Beebe had not only become known for his speed and integrity, he had a wacky sense of humor that earned him good ratings in markets that loved their NFL teams. Both shows, in Wisconsin and New York, shared formats that began with the host's monologues; then he introduced off-the-wall segments and guests that included everyone from the rap group Run-DMC to billiards queen Ewa Lawrence.

Beebe's out-on-the-town segments were equally diverse: walleye fishing one week, man-on-the-streets the next. And, in addition to the Halloween prank, there was plenty of Packers footage, including one of Beebe's favorites, with strong safety LeRoy Butler, after he'd just signed a five-year contract extension with the Packers for $15 million.

Beebe chatted with the Pro-Bowler — credited with creating the Lambeau Leap when he jumped into the stands in 1993 after forcing a fumble — for a few minutes about his new contract. Then Don aired a video of his visit to a local bank the day before, where the talk-show host and his camera crew were escorted into the vault to film a large pile of money stacked on a table. Beebe could be seen looking earnestly into the camera. "You see this tall stack of bills? This is how much money LeRoy just signed for."

Then the camera swiveled to the right, to a pathetic stack of silver quarters. Beebe moved from behind the mountain of bills to the small pile of coins. "And this is how much Don Beebe makes," he deadpanned.

Those who knew Beebe and his aversion to public speaking from years ago could never have imagined him being so comfortable in front of a camera that he could host his own television show. But those same people also knew there were many layers to the deeply intense athlete not necessarily evident when he was competing on the field. He could be mischievous without being mean, droll without being sarcastic. And his humbleness made it easy for him to poke fun at himself, as well as those around him. Early on in his career, he'd become the butt of his teammates' jokes after showing up at a team dinner his rookie year wearing a cheap suit jacket so short he looked more like a maître' d than Buffalo's top draft pick.

But his ability to take, as well as give, a good joke was a quality that endeared him to the fans he impressed on Sunday afternoons. "I have my good days and my bad days, like everyone else," he once told a reporter. "But even on my bad days I'm still the same person. My faith gives me an inner peace that helps me get through a lot.

"And if you have that, even on those bad days, you still can find a reason to laugh."

Some days, that was easier said than done; at least for Diana.

CHAPTER 31 – Doing What It Takes

No matter which stadium she was sitting in, no matter what row her seat, Don's wife could always hear the crunch that sent him to the turf.

In this match-up against Detroit, it was no different. Beebe cut across the middle in the red zone, just three plays into the second quarter, and got nailed on the one-yard line after snagging the short pass from Favre.

Diana saw Don fold over. She couldn't bear to look up at the Jumbo Tron that zoomed in on his body, lying motionless for what seemed like an eternity. In reality, he was down for only a few seconds. But as Don got up and limped toward the sideline, Diana could sense he was having trouble breathing. It was close to halftime so her anxious heart had time to take a quick rest before the third quarter started. But it picked up its rapid-fire rhythm when she saw her husband trot back out on the field.

There was reason for her concern. Halfway through that quarter, Detroit's Bennie Blades caught Don square in the head, and knocked him so hard, it required smelling salts to bring him back around. The team doctor, Pat McKenzie, checked Don out, but it was head trainer Pepper Burress who broke the news. "You're done, Don. You're not going back out there again."

Knowing Beebe, Burress turned to Red Batty, the head equipment man. "Hide his helmet," he ordered. "He's done for the day."

Don wasn't happy. When he realized the coaches were benching him, he combed the sidelines in search of the missing helmet. He checked under the benches. He rummaged through piles of warm-up jackets.

Within five minutes, he found what he was looking for — under the tarp that covered the instant-replay camera.

With no one paying much attention, Beebe rammed the helmet back on his head, and at the end of the next play, jogged back onto the field. "I'm in for you," he announced to rookie Derrick Mayes.

When the trainer saw Beebe heading for the huddle, he threw his hands in the air and yelled at Holmgren. "What's Beebs doing out there? He's not supposed to be playing."

The head coach shrugged. "He's fine," he said. "Let him go."

Witnessing it all from the fifth row along the thirty-five-yard line, Diana shuddered. Then she prayed.

Back in the huddle, Favre called for a play-action fake the team had created for this week only. Favre pretended to hand off the ball to the fullback, but instead, the QB dropped back, throwing the ball to Beebe who was running a fly pattern to the strong side. Diana could barely force herself to watch. Favre launched the ball and she held her breath as Don leaped off the ground to snare the catch. Sixty-five yards later, Don crossed the goal line, sealing Green Bay's victory over the Lions.

"Don't hit him in the head!" yelled Burress, as the Packers high-fived and slapped each other in celebration of No. 82's touchdown.

Beebe grinned at the head trainer. "I told you not to hide my helmet," he said.

Later, Don confessed to Diana he couldn't even remember catching that long pass. And her prayers grew more desperate. At the same time, she also realized it was this exasperating brand of spunkiness that made Don a favorite with Green Bay's blue-collar fans.

Known for their own work ethic, Cheeseheads everywhere had a new underdog to root for. Don Beebe truly was their Little Engine that Could, and fans ate it up. It didn't hurt that Beebs, whenever he had the chance, talked about how important it was to be a team player. The Packers were as close to a Super Bowl appearance as they'd been in years. And he wanted to help them attain that goal, even if it meant returning kickoffs or taking passes in traffic.

In 1996 regular season play, the Packers posted a 13-3 record, earning them a bye the first week of the playoffs and home-field advantage for the remaining games. And that advantage was especially important for the Packers on the aptly nicknamed "Frozen Tundra" of Lambeau Field. They won handily over the 49ers on a rain-soaked muddy turf. Then, in the NFC Championship game, the Packers dismantled the Carolina Panthers, the team that cut Beebe from the roster the previous year. But revenge was far from his mind: He had nothing but respect for Polian and Coach Dom Capers, who had managed to take this young team to the playoffs in its second year in existence.

After twenty-nine years, the Lombardi Trophy, awarded to the NFL champions, had an excellent chance of returning to the home of its namesake. But first, the Packers had to beat the New England Patriots, surprise winners of the AFC.

CHAPTER 32 –Winning, Finally

For the fifth time, Don Beebe was going to play in the Super Bowl, four more than most of the players on the team. In fact, he and backup quarterback Jim McMahon, who engineered the Chicago Bears Super Bowl XX championship in January 1986, were the only players who had ever been to the big game.

"I can't stress enough how important it is to stay focused on the game," Don told his teammates, as they prepared for Super Bowl XXXI. "Whatever you do, don't get caught up in the hype; don't forget why you are here. And please, guys, let your wives or someone else handle all the calls that are going to be coming in from the entire world wanting tickets."

Beebe was, as always, hit with his share of requests from family, friends and casual acquaintances who wanted to be in the stands in New Orleans. Buffalo had usually handed out about thirty Super Bowl tickets to each player, but with Green Bay, there was only a stingy fifteen. That meant plenty of requests he couldn't accommodate. But this year he made sure the list included his childhood buddies, Jim and Jeff Still. Only six months earlier, Jeff, a young husband and father to two little boys, had committed himself to Jesus Christ, and Beebe could see the profound change in the man. But somehow, in a mix-up they never could figure out, the Still brothers were excluded from those guest passes — a fact the Beebes were mortified to discover two days before the game.

"Don't sweat it, Beebs," Jeff told his longtime buddy, that ever-present grin masking the disappointment he must surely have felt. "I know how crazy it's been for you. Jim and I will just hang out in the hotel and watch the game on TV."

Beebe was frustrated. "Is there any way we can get tickets for them?" he asked Diana. "Maybe some other players have extras."

His wife shook her head. "Not at this late date. I don't think we're going to be able to come up with a ticket unless someone isn't using theirs."

Then an idea hit her: "Why don't I give up my seat? I've already been to four Super Bowls and at least one of them could see the game instead of watching it from some hotel room."

Don knew his wife was serious but he couldn't go along with the suggestion. For one thing, he couldn't imagine either of the brothers taking the ticket and leaving the other behind. Plus, Diana had to be in the stands for this game.

"This time, we're going to win it all," he said. "Besides, I have a feeling it will somehow get resolved. Let's just see how this plays out."

Thirty-six hours before kickoff, Beebe's dad called. "Son, I hate to tell you this, but your mom still isn't feeling any better. That bug she came down with isn't giving up. I'm afraid she won't be able to make it to New Orleans. And I don't want to leave her alone. Is there someone else you could give our tickets to?"

As much as he loved his dad, Don couldn't get him off the phone fast enough. "Make sure you and Jim buy yourselves some nice new Green Bay shirts, bro," he told Jeff on the phone a minute later. "Because I expect you two to be yelling louder than anyone else in the stadium."

The night before the game, Don and the Still brothers, along with their good friend Mike Walker, had the time of their lives exploring downtown New Orleans. After filling their stomachs with jambalaya and shrimp Creole, the four men, buddies since grade school, found a Nerf football in Walker's car, and as they strolled down the middle of Bourbon

Street, Jeff suggested they re-enact a few plays they were convinced would take place in the Louisiana Superdome on the following day.

Only, in this game, Jeff was the receiver. And as he was going down, out and up for a pass, the two defenders, Jim Still and Walker, fell for the fake. That's when Jeff broke clear on the up, and Don, acting as quarterback, laid a perfectly thrown spiral over his friend's left shoulder.

"Touchdown! Six points!" shouted Jeff, as he ran past the imaginary goal line, a fire hydrant sporting a Packer's ski hat.

"Nice fake," laughed Don. "Let's hope we have that same kind of luck against two defensive backs who don't have lead in their pants."

Later, before the Stills dropped Don off at the players' hotel, Jeff admitted to Don how much happier he was, in all aspects of life, since accepting Jesus into his heart. "I love working with kids," said the middle school teacher and coach. "And I want to find ways to mentor them more. There are so many young people struggling out there right now. I look around and I see the pain in their faces. These guys didn't do anything to deserve what's happening to them. They have it rough, Don. And I want to help them find a way to get through it all, to give them some hope."

"You will," his buddy told him. "You are in such a good place now."

Jeff was in a good place the following day, too — right on the forty-five-yard line for Super Bowl XXXI. And he and his brother, faces painted in Green Bay colors, cheered louder than anyone as the Packers got off to a strong start against New England with a fifty-four-yard touchdown pass from Favre to Andre Rison.

That score was quickly followed by a Green Bay field goal after a turnover by the Patriots. Then New England scored back-to-back touchdowns within a matter of minutes, giving the Patriots a 14-10 lead at the end of the first quarter. But unlike Beebe's other Super Bowl team, the

Packers didn't come unglued upon facing a little adversity on the big stage. Favre, always cool under fire, hit Freeman with an eighty-one-yard touchdown pass, then the Packers came back with another Chris Jacke field goal. After Mark Prior intercepted Drew Bledsoe, the Packers scored on a two-yard touchdown run to take a 27-14 lead into the locker at halftime.

Curtis Martin cut the Packers' lead to 27-21 with an eighteen-yard touchdown run in the third quarter. But New England's hopes were diminished when Desmond Howard returned the following kickoff ninety-nine yards for a touchdown. Favre hit tight end Mark Chmura with the two-point conversion to put the Packers back up 35-21 going into the final quarter.

There was no scoring in the fourth. And as the smell of a Green Bay victory grew stronger with every minute that evaporated on the scoreboard, Jeff Still grabbed Diana and pulled her into a bear hug that she would feel for the next 24 hours. Brett Favre took a knee, and the Packers had themselves a Super Bowl victory.

Don Beebe, the veteran wide receiver, hadn't caught a pass in this monumental win, but you couldn't tell it by the of joy on his face. Antonio Freeman, Andre Rison and Desmond Howard, the game's MVP, had all scored their first Super Bowl touchdowns, and Don, remembering his own with the Bills, knew how special this moment was for them.

As bedlam broke out, with players, coaches, photographers, reporters and even the fans swarming the field, Beebe approached Favre, who was still holding on to the game ball. Don thought about all those years walking off the fields dejected in those crushing Super Bowl defeats with the Bills. He thought about those many months of pounding his leg up a steep hill to repair his shattered bone. About playing at tiny Chadron

State in the prairies of northwest Nebraska. About nearly killing himself on ladders while hanging aluminum siding.

He thought about Melissa, still courageously battling her disease as only the smallest can. About Jeff Still, dancing wildly in the stands right now, and how his love for Jesus had transformed his heart.

And he remembered the little boy from Sugar Grove running, catching and passing those dog-eared footballs as he mangled his parent's back yard so many years ago.

"Do you think I could have the game ball?" he asked Favre. "I'd really like to have it for my family."

The quarterback, who would go on to be named the NFL's Most Valuable Player two years in a row, didn't hesitate. He grinned and flipped the ball toward his receiver.

"Sure thing," he said. "You deserve it, Beebs."

EPILOGUE – Building On New Ground

Anticipation hung over the locker room like a heavy stage curtain about to rise on a long-awaited drama. Under the dim lighting, young warriors — red and blue armor exaggerating their fierceness — readied for battle. A few, clutching helmets and nervous stomachs, paced the carpeted floor. Many appeared motionless, some leaning against a wall, heads back, dark-painted eyes raised skyward. Others sat like statues on the unforgiving benches, their bodies hunched over turf-scraped hands folded in prayer.

Over in the far left corner, a circle of five huddled closely, shoulders touching as the tallest led them in verses from the book of Psalms. And against this background, a CD player spun, filling the room with The Katinas' "Thank You."

Just a little while longer I wanna pray;
Can't get You off my mind so I came to say
Thank You Lord just for loving me.
Many times as I do forget
Every need that You have met ...

It was almost time. In a few minutes the Eagles from Aurora Christian High School would quietly file through the dark tunnel — cleats click-click-clicking on the cold November cement — and explode onto the artificial turf of the University of Illinois' Memorial Stadium.

It was Thanksgiving weekend, and in the stands, some two thousand fans waved signs, clutched hot chocolate and tried to quiet their

208

own butterflies as they waited for the teams to take the field in this 2008 Illinois High School Class 4A state championship game.

The Eagles' opponent — Bloomington Central Catholic — was bigger, stronger, and after three state titles in the last five years, decidedly more experienced. Some called it a David-and-Goliath match-up. Others weren't about to sell short this small group of underdogs from Aurora who had managed to manhandle plenty of oversized teams on their march through the Illinois High School Association playoffs. The Eagles, according to the hometown sports section, had tenacity and surprising quickness.

And they could boast of a head coach who'd used those same qualities to collect more Super Bowl rings than any other NFL player.

* * *

In 1997, his ninth season in the NFL, Don Beebe had asked God again to point the way. "Lord, if you want this to be my last year, you have to delete the passion," he had prayed. A few weeks after the Packers' Super Bowl XXXI win, the Beebes were celebrating on a cruise in the Virgin Islands when Don received an emergency phone call.

"Son," his mother greeted him, the sorrow in her voice apparent, "I'm sorry to have to interrupt your vacation, but Jeff Still was killed in a car accident last night. He was hit by a drunk driver."

The couple immediately flew home. Within weeks, Don recruited NFL buddies Jim Kelly, Reggie White and Desmond Howard to hold a football camp fundraiser for Jeff's widow and two young sons. It was good to see his Bills buddies again. But his childhood friend's needless death had taken something out of him. And the dark days only continued.

The following January, the Packers made it back to the championship game, which would now give Don Beebe a record six Super Bowl rings. It had not been a good year for the thirty-three-year-old wide receiver, however. Don struggled through a season riddled with injuries, including another major concussion. But he promised Coach Holmgren he'd be ready for the Super Bowl; and that first practice in San Diego, where the Packers would take on the Broncos, had gone exceptionally well for him.

That next morning, Holmgren called him down to the breakfast lobby in the Hyatt Regency. Green Bay's head coach promised he'd keep it short, then told Don he wouldn't be suiting up for the Super Bowl. The Packers had decided to go with Ronnie Anderson, a younger player who had promise. They didn't want to lose a chance at signing the kid next year.

Holmgren might as well have taken an arrow and driven it through Don's heart.

Green Bay lost to Denver 31-24 in Super Bowl XXXII on January 25, 1998. Two weeks later, the rookie they'd been courting was cut from the team. And the Packers didn't renew Beebe's contract. Although Don had a chance to sign on with Oakland, he realized this setback was what he needed to move on with his life. That May, Beebe announced his retirement from the NFL and moved his family back to the Sugar Grove area. There, he started House of Speed, a sports training facility for young athletes. But as much as he loved the academy, he realized his calling was to work with kids on a more personal level.

As it turned out, Leon Lett, the man so vilified after that famous Super Bowl play, followed that same calling, as his life continued to parallel Beebe's own. The Big Cat faced some challenges after that day. But like Don, he began mentoring kids, not only in his hometown, but also in Las Vegas, where he was named Ambassador to the Rainbow Dreams Charter School.

Also like Don, he turned that one Super Bowl moment into a powerful teaching tool. Only, his lesson was formed through a different perspective. "It helped me grow as a person," he told Beebe when the two met almost 20 years later, "because I wanted to prove I was more than that one bad play. It gave me a burning passion to prove everyone wrong."

And he continues to use that passion to help kids remember the importance of "always finishing what you start so you don't have to spend the rest of your life living with regret."

It was the same message Don relied on throughout his life as he struggled with major decisions. They were words that guided him when he began fielding six-figure coaching offers from professional and college teams. As tempting as these job offers were, he knew he'd feel regret if he went in that direction. Instead, he was pulled toward Aurora Christian, a school of four hundred students whose football team, with a record of 21-36 in its six-year history, didn't even have its own stadium.

When he heard the school was moving into an old warehouse on Sullivan Road, with the goal of someday building a field on the vacant lot behind the building, he decided to stop by the new site on his way home from a movie with Diana. A few minutes later, Beebe found himself kneeling on that rocky, weedy patch of ground that would someday be the fifty-yard-line. "Lord, if this is where you want me," he prayed, "I'm yours."

As he felt the tugging of the spirit again, Don was overcome with emotion. Tears filling his eyes, he walked back to the car, where his wife had been waiting patiently.

"Diana," he said, "I'm going to be the next football coach here."

Despite his nine years in the NFL, Don was hardly a rich man. Most of the money he had invested was gone; with the financial adviser he thought was his friend now serving prison time after swindling Beebe and a host of other athletes out of their life savings. Still, Beebe surprised Aurora Christian by refusing a salary. And there was never any talk about money — except when it came to the football field the school and coach were determined to build. One generous donor and an entire community rallied behind this improbable cause, and within six months, the school had raised $1 million for a new state-of-the-art stadium.

But Beebe, as excited as he was about the construction project, was more interested in building young men.

*　*　*

Here I am with all I am;
Raise my hands to worship You.
We wanna say thank you, oh thank you
For everything ...

Beebe strolled to the center of the Eagles locker room and muted The Katinas' melody. "Let's bring it in, guys," he called out to the team. Wordlessly, forty-three players floated toward their coach and formed a semicircle around him. As their eyes locked on his, Beebe was taken aback by the trust he saw in these young faces. All year long, the teenagers had done what he asked them to do: study hard, practice hard and lead a Christian-filled life.

Jordan Roberts, his star quarterback had already shattered a few IHSA records, including more than ten thousand career yards. The kid was a star, no doubt about it. But mostly he was a role model who showed that leadership off the field is as important as on it.

Lewis Gaddis enrolled at Aurora Christian as a teenage father with club feet and a poor attitude. Four years under Beebe, he was now one of the quickest, most effective running backs in the conference. And even more importantly, he had stepped up to relish his responsibility to his young family.

Hunter Taylor, a second-string lineman with Asperger syndrome, transferred from a large public school after he'd been mercilessly teased and bullied by the players on his former team. When his mother had heard about Beebe's program, she decided making the forty-five minute drive every day to Aurora was worth the sacrifice.

That's because Beebe's football program was about more than play patterns and strength conditioning. He led Bible studies every week in the weight room. He held a senior-night bonfire at the beginning of the season; and later a father-son retreat, where dialogues and hearts were opened, some for the first time. Yet the players also realized early on their coach was an intense competitor with a no-nonsense style. If players didn't complete homework, they ran laps. If grades slipped below 80 percent, they were hit with mandatory study hall. Any failing grades meant they were ineligible to play that week.

"Because of you, Coach, my son has a future. He has hope," Hunter's grateful mom told him the night the Eagles clinched the win in the state semifinals.

Now, on this cold November evening, the only lessons would be taken from a hard-fought battle. For Beebe, there was little left to say, except a reminder of why they were here.

"From the rocks, weeds and mud that used to be your football field, we've come a long way, boys. Win or lose, you will always be winners in my heart. You have honored God with your play, you have led by example, and many have taken notice. We pray for victory but if it is not God's will, we will fight to the end."

The young warriors nodded their heads as they drew closer to their coach. They watched his eyes grow darker. "Now, let's go win a state championship."

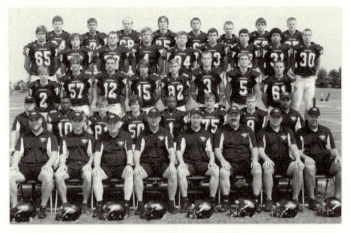

Aurora Christian's Illinois 3A 2011 Champions
Photos courtesy of Dan Anderson

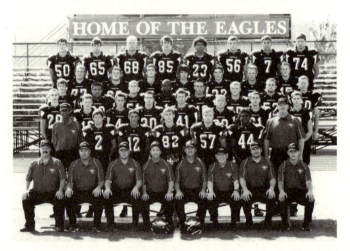

On November 23, 2012
Aurora Christian repeats as Illinois 3A 2012 Champions

EXTRA POINT

Champaign – They were denied, but not in denial. Aurora Christian came up short in its bid to bring home the first state football title to the city of Aurora, but the Eagles teamed up with Bloomington Central Catholic to put on an entertaining display of offensive fireworks Friday before falling 37-28.

The Aurora Beacon-News story that ran Nov. 29, 2008, went on to describe how, despite Jordan Roberts' 300 throwing yards and four scores, the Eagles could not keep up with the Saints in this offensive showdown that featured a combined 892 yards of offense.

Disappointed but keeping their eye on the goal, Don Beebe and his team marched down state again three years later. And on Thanksgiving weekend in 2011, they finally brought home Aurora's first state championship trophy after soundly beating Mt. Carmel 34-7.

This time, it was quarterback Anthony Maddie's talents that led the Eagles to this historic win. The senior ran for three touchdowns and threw for another two, accumulating 285 total yards. But it was a team effort for Aurora Christian. Players saw more than their share of injuries and other adversities throughout the 13-1 season. And it was the way the boys responded to their many hurdles that made their coach so proud as he stood atop the stage in Champaign that Friday night and watched his captains hoist the trophy high into the air.

"Any time you're the first in history, that's big," Beebe told reporters at the post-game press conference, referring to the city's only football title. "Coaching the state championship team was way better than winning the Super Bowl."

ABOUT THE AUTHOR

Photo Credit: Sun-Times Media

Denise Crosby is a former teacher, author and award-winning journalist who has spent the last 30 years chasing after stories and her six children. Raised on a wheat and cattle farm, she graduated with honors from Kansas State University. Her writing, recognized on a state and national level dozens of times, include multiple Peter Lisagor Awards presented by the Chicago Headline Club; and back-to-back Illinois Associated Press Sweepstakes honors. Denise is senior columnist for Sun-Times Media West and lives in suburban Chicago with her husband, a growing number of pets and declining number of kids. As the mother of a half-dozen athletes involved in sports from T-ball to professional ball, she knows her way around plenty of fields and stadiums.